AMPHIGOREY

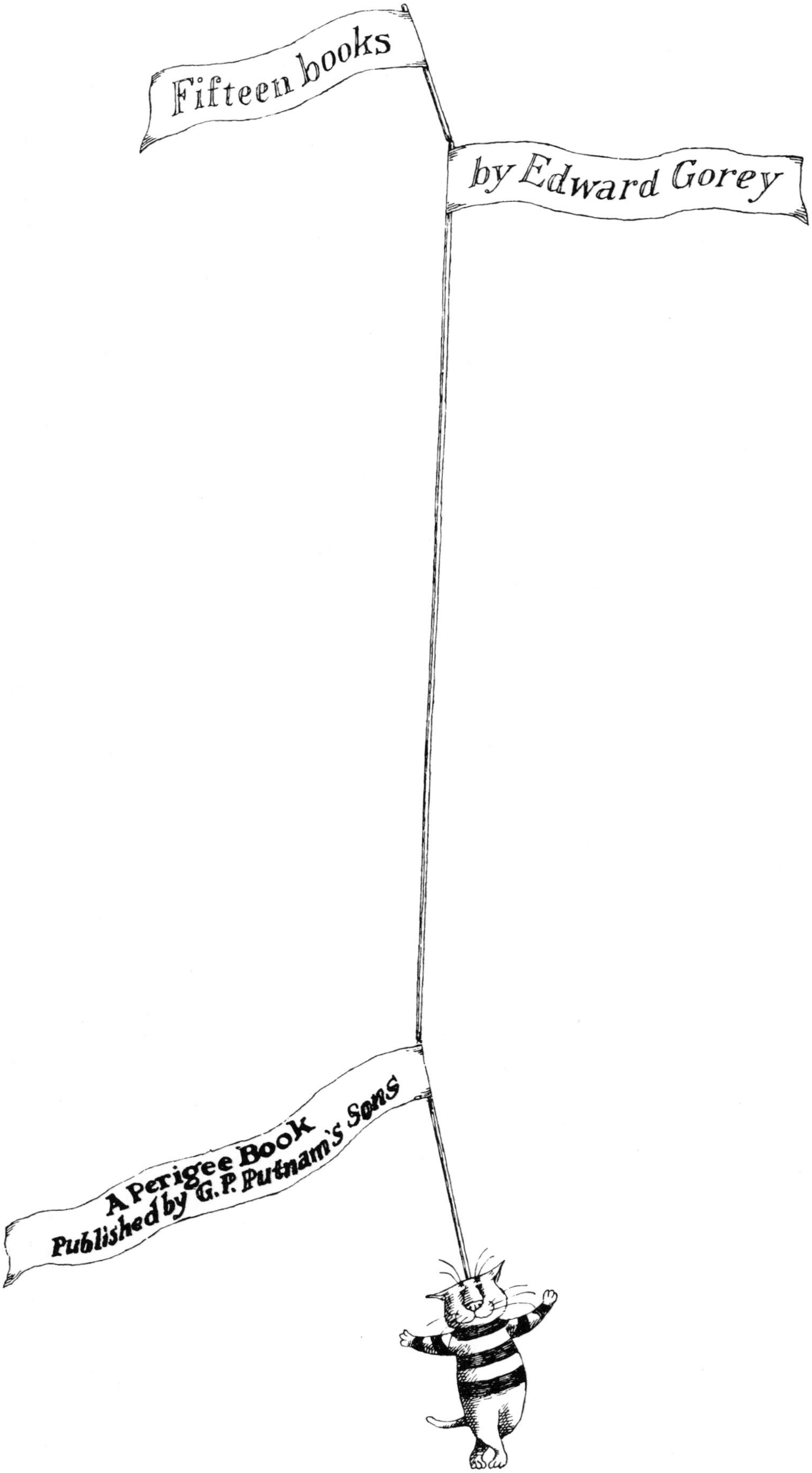
Fifteen books
by Edward Gorey
A Perigee Book
Published by G. P. Putnam's Sons

A
M
P
H
I
G
O
R
E
Y

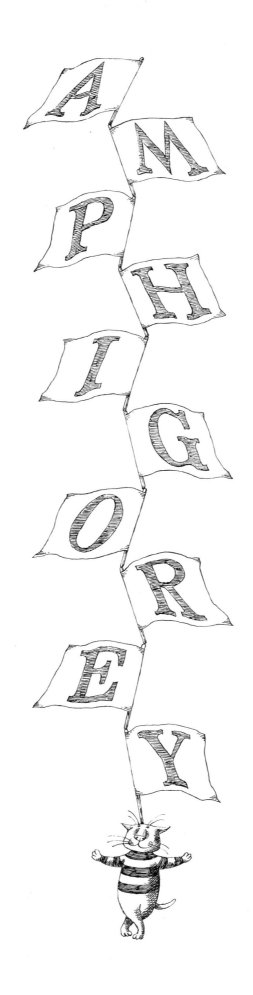

Published simultaneously in Canada by Academic Press Canada Limited, Toronto.

ISBN: 0-399-50433-8

Perigee Books
are published by
G.P. Putnam Sons
200 Madison Avenue
New York, N.Y. 10016

Five Previous Paperback Printings
First Perigee Printing, 1981

8   9   10

The works in the present volume were first published as indicated:
The Unstrung Harp, 1953, *The Listing Attic*, 1954, Duell, Sloan and Pearce-Little Brown;
The Doubtful Guest, 1957, *The Object-Lesson*, 1958, Doubleday & Company, Inc.;
The Bug Book, 1960, Epstein & Carroll; *The Fatal Lozenge*, 1960, *The Hapless Child*, 1961,
The Curious Sofa, 1961, *The Sinking Spell*, 1964, Ivan Obolensky, Inc.; *The Willowdale
Handcar*, 1962, The Bobbs-Merrill Company Inc.; *The Wuggly Ump*, 1963, J.B. Lippincott
Company; *The Gashlycrumb Tinies*, 1963, *The Insect God*, 1963, *The West Wing*, 1963,
The Remembered Visit, 1965, Simon and Schuster. The author and publisher
acknowledge with special thanks all courtesies of the foregoing publishers.

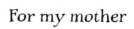
For my mother

Amphigorey is made up of books first published between 1953 and 1965. They are now difficult and often expensive to come by: hence this compilation. Its title is taken from amphigory, or amphigouri, meaning a nonsense verse or composition.

E.G.

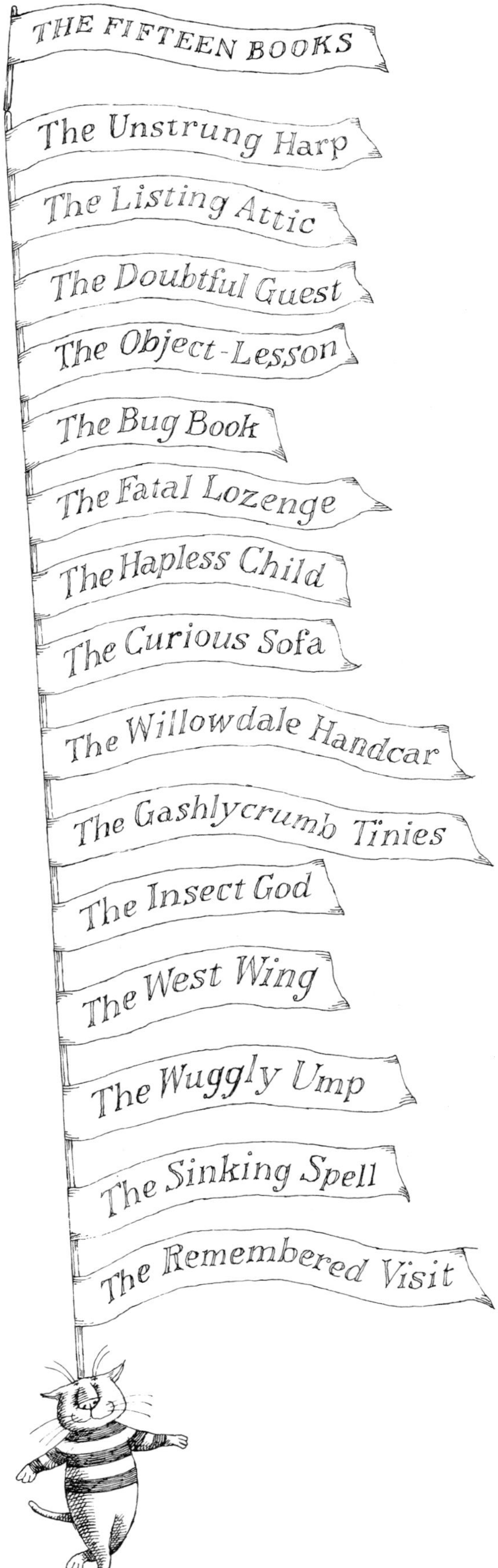
THE FIFTEEN BOOKS
The Unstrung Harp
The Listing Attic
The Doubtful Guest
The Object-Lesson
The Bug Book
The Fatal Lozenge
The Hapless Child
The Curious Sofa
The Willowdale Handcar
The Gashlycrumb Tinies
The Insect God
The West Wing
The Wuggly Ump
The Sinking Spell
The Remembered Visit

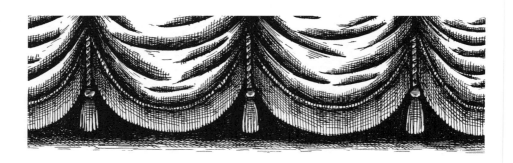

Mr Gorey, Mr Earbrass, and a Knowledgeable Friend.

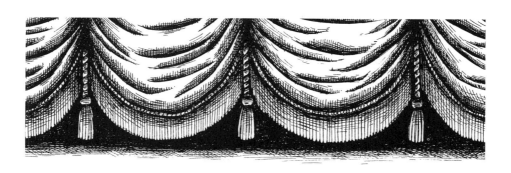

The
Unstrung
Harp;

or, Mr Earbrass Writes a Novel.

Mr C(lavius) F(rederick) Earbrass is, of course, the well-known novelist. Of his books, *A Moral Dustbin, More Chains Than Clank, Was It Likely?,* and the Hipdeep trilogy are, perhaps, the most admired. Mr Earbrass is seen on the croquet lawn of his home, Hobbies Odd, near Collapsed Pudding in Mortshire. He is studying a game left unfinished at the end of summer.

On November 18th of alternate years Mr Earbrass begins writing 'his new novel'. Weeks ago he chose its title at random from a list of them he keeps in a little green note-book. It being tea-time of the 17th, he is alarmed not to have thought of a plot to which *The Unstrung Harp* might apply, but his mind will keep reverting to the last biscuit on the plate.

Snow was falling when Mr Earbrass woke, which suggested he open *TUH* with the first flakes of what could be developed into a prolonged and powerfully purple blizzard. On paper, if not outdoors, they have kept coming down all afternoon, over and over again, in all possible ways; and only now, at nightfall, have done so satisfactorily. For writing Mr Earbrass affects an athletic sweater of forgotten origin and unknown significance; it is always worn hind-side-to.

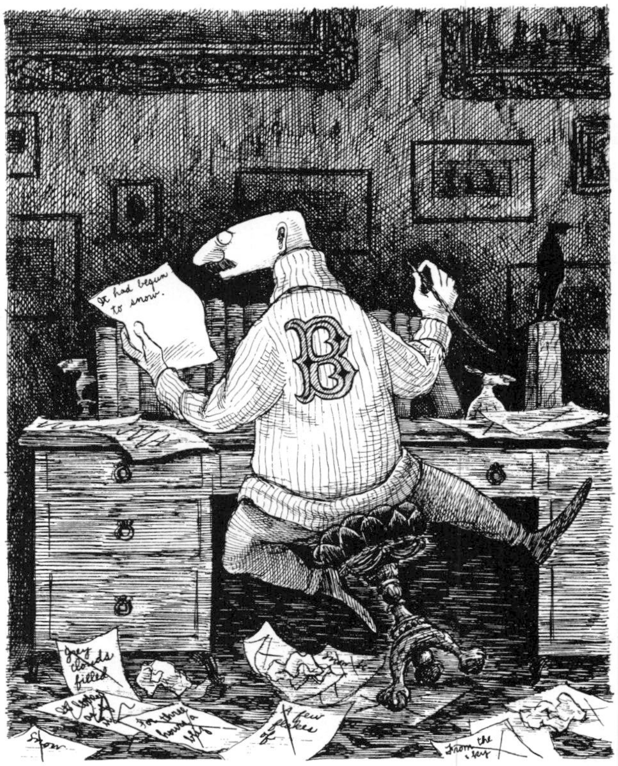
It had begun to snow.
grey clouds filled
For three hours a
A few flakes
Snow
from the sky

Several weeks later, the loofah trickling on his knees, Mr Earbrass mulls over an awkward retrospective bit that ought to go in Chapter II. But where? Even the voice of the omniscient author can hardly afford to interject a seemingly pointless anecdote concerning Ladderback in Tibet when the other characters are feverishly engaged in wondering whether to have the pond at Disshiver Cottage dragged or not.

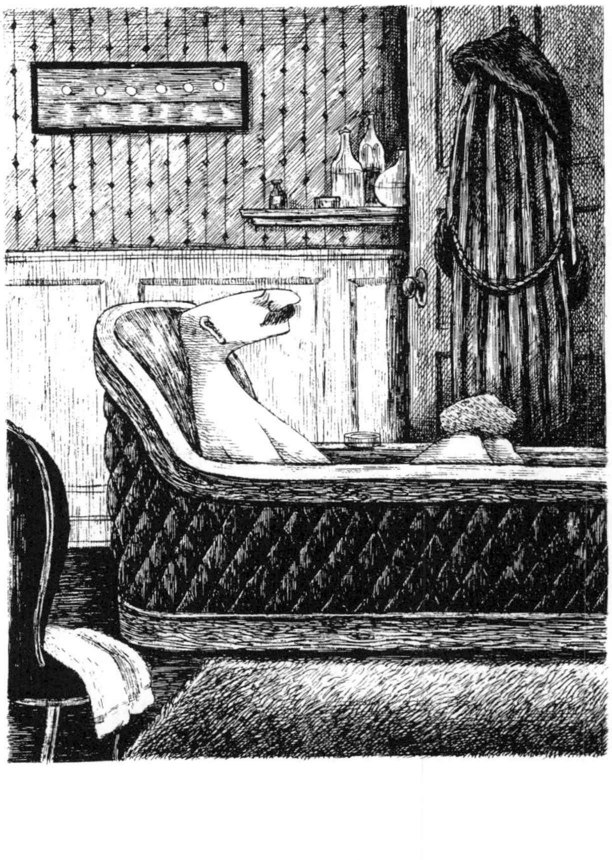

Mr Earbrass belongs to the straying, rather than to the sedentary, type of author. He is never to be found at his desk unless actually writing down a sentence. Before this happens he broods over it indefinitely while picking up and putting down again small, loose objects; walking diagonally across rooms; staring out windows; and so forth. He frequently hums, more in his mind than anywhere else, themes from the Poddington *Te Deum*.

It was one of Mr Earbrass's better days; he wrote for so long and with such intensity that when he stopped he felt quite sick. Having leaned out a window into a strong wind for several minutes, he is now restoring himself in the kitchen and rereading *TUH* as far as he has gotten. He cannot help but feel that Lirp's return and almost immediate impalement on the bottle-tree was one of his better ideas. The jelly in his sandwich is about to get all over his fingers.

Mr Earbrass has finished Chapter VII, and it is obvious that before plunging ahead himself he has got to decide where the plot is to go and what will happen to it on arrival. He is engaged in making diagrams of possible routes and destinations, and wishing he had not dealt so summarily with Lirp, who would have been useful for taking retributive measures at the end of Part Three. At the moment there is no other character capable of them.

Out for a short drive before a supper of oysters and trifle, Mr Earbrass stops near the abandoned fireworks factory outside Something Awful. There is a drowned sort of yellow light in the west, and the impression of desolation and melancholy is remarkable. Mr Earbrass jots down a few visual notes he suspects may be useful when he reaches the point where the action of *TUW* shifts to Hangdog Hall.

Mr Earbrass was virtually asleep when several lines of verse passed through his mind and left it hopelessly awake. Here was the perfect epigraph for *TUH*:

A horrid ?monster has been [something]
delay'd
By your/their indiff'rence in the dank
brown shade
Below the garden...

His mind's eye sees them quoted on the bottom third of a right-hand page in a (possibly) olive-bound book he read at least five years ago. When he does find them, it will be a great nuisance if no clue is given to their authorship.

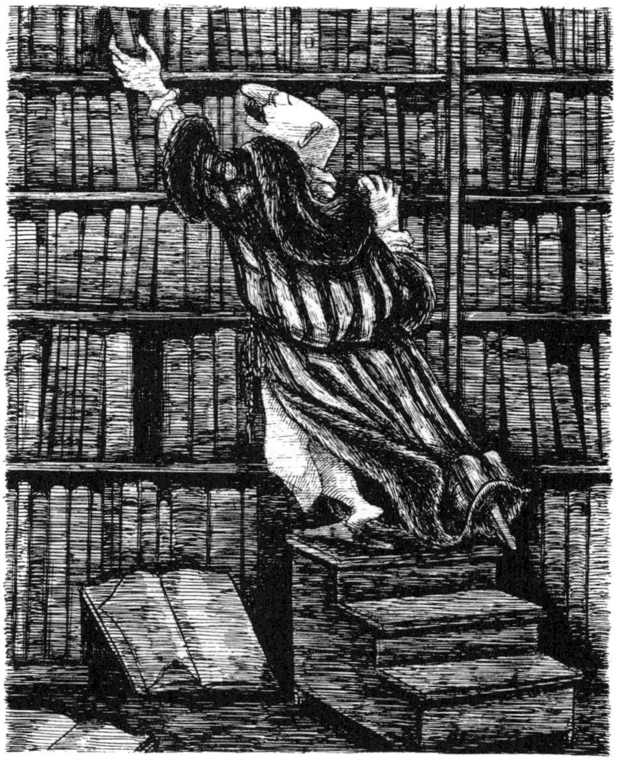

Mr Earbrass has driven over to Nether Millstone in search of forced greengages, but has been distracted by a bookseller's. Rummaging among mostly religious tracts and privately printed reminiscences, he has come across *The Meaning of the House*, his second novel. In making sure it has not got there by mistake (as he would hardly care to pay more for it), he discovers it is a presentation copy. *For Angus—will you ever forget the bloaters?* Bloaters? Angus?

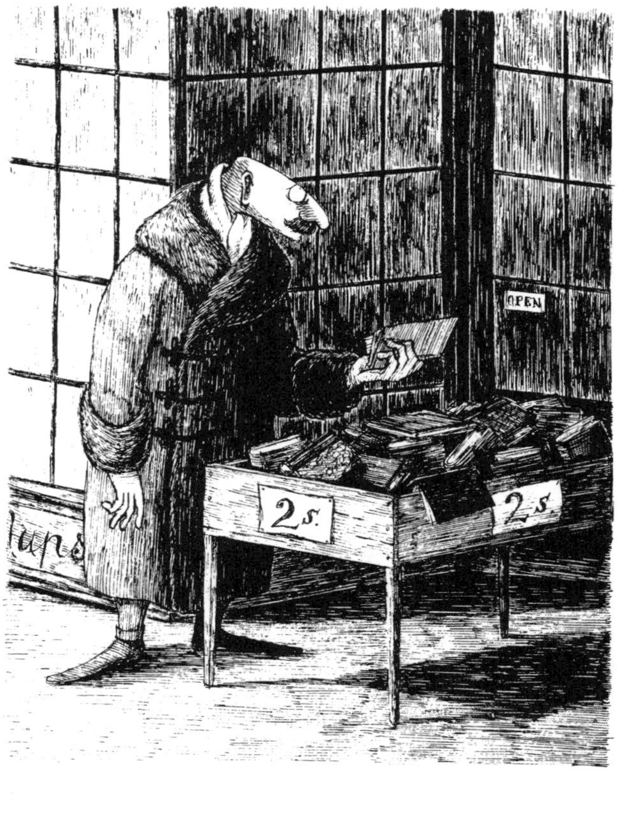
OPEN
2s.
2s.

The first draft of *TUH* is more than half
finished, and for some weeks its characters
have been assuming a fitful and cloudy
reality. Now a minor one named Glassglue
has materialized at the head of the stairs
as his creator is about to go down to dinner.
Mr Earbrass was aware of the peculiarly
unpleasant nubs on his greatcoat, but not the
blue-tinted spectacles. Glassglue is about to
mutter something in a tone too low to be
caught and, stepping sideways, vanish.

Mr Earbrass has been rashly skimming
through the early chapters, which he has not
looked at for months, and now sees *TUH* for
what it is. Dreadful, *dreadful*, DREADFUL. He
must be mad to go on enduring the unexquisite
agony of writing when it all turns out drivel.
Mad. Why didn't he become a spy? How does
one become one? He will burn the MS. Why
is there no fire? Why aren't there the
makings of one? How did he get in the
unused room on the third floor?

Mr Earbrass returned from a walk to find a large carton blocking the hall. Masses of brow paper and then tissue have reluctantly given up an unnerving silver-gilt combination epergne and candelabrum. Mr Earbrass recollects a letter from a hitherto unknown admirer of his work, received the week before; it hinted at the early arrival of an offering that embodied, in a different but kindred form, the same high-souled aspiration that animated its recipient's books. Mr Earbrass can only conclude that the apathy of the lower figures is due to their having been deprived of novels.

Even more harrowing than the first chapters of a novel are the last, for Mr Earbrass anyway. The characters have one and all become thoroughly tiresome, as though he had been trapped at the same party with them since the day before; neglected sections of the plot loom on every hand, waiting to be disposed of; his verbs seem to have withered away and his adjectives to be proliferating past control. Furthermore, at this stage he inevitably gets insomnia. Even rereading *The Truffle Plantation* (his first novel) does not induce sleep. In the blue horror of dawn the vines in the carpet appear likely to begin twining up his ankles.

Though *TUH* is within less than a chapter of completion, Mr Earbrass has felt it his cultural and civic duty, and a source of possible edification, to attend a performance at Lying-in-the-Way of Prawne's *The Nephew's Tragedy*. It is being put on, for the first time since the early seventeenth century, by the West Mortshire Impassioned Amateurs of Melpomene. Unfortunately, Mr Earbrass is unable to take in even one of its five plots because he cannot get those few unwritten pages out of his mind.

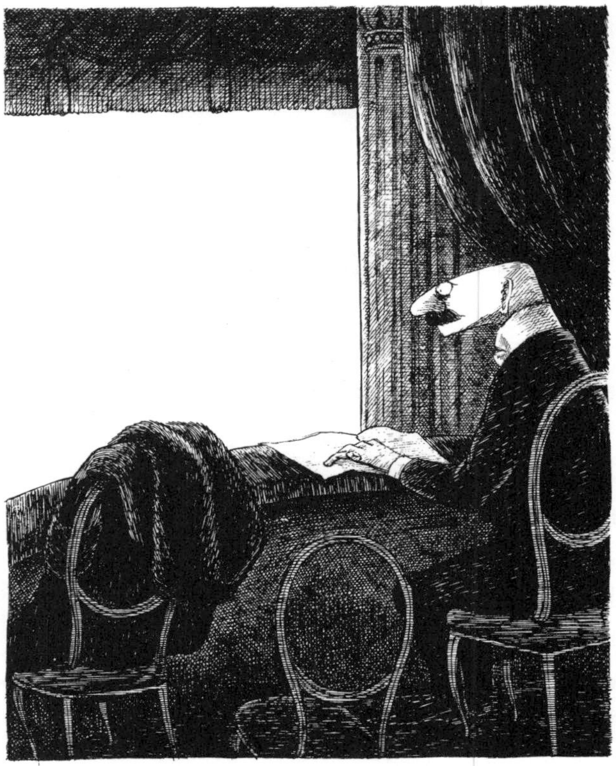

In that brief moment between day and night when everything seems to have stopped for good and all, Mr Earbrass has written the last sentence of *TUH*. The room's appearance of tidiness and Mr Earbrass's of calm are alike deceptive. The MS is stuffed all anyhow in the lower right-hand drawer of the desk and Mr Earbrass himself is wildly distrait. His feet went to sleep some time ago, there is a dull throbbing behind his left ear, and his moustache feels as uncomfortable as if it were false, or belonged to someone else.

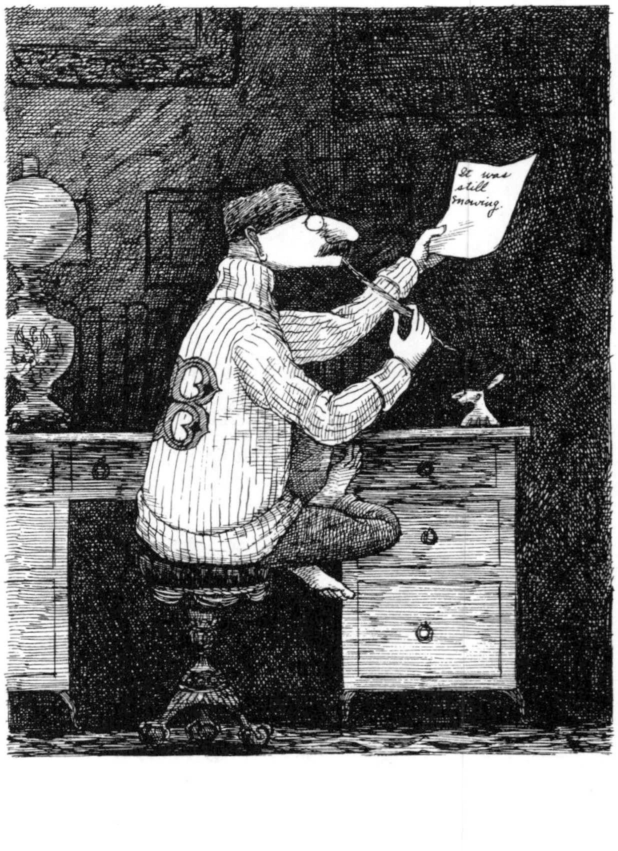
It was still snowing.

The next day Mr Earbrass is conscious but very little more. He wanders through the house, leaving doors open and empty tea-cups on the floor. From time to time the thought occurs to him that he really ought to go and dress, and he gets up several minutes later, only to sit down again in the first chair he comes to. The better part of a week will have elapsed before he has recovered enough to do anything more helpful.

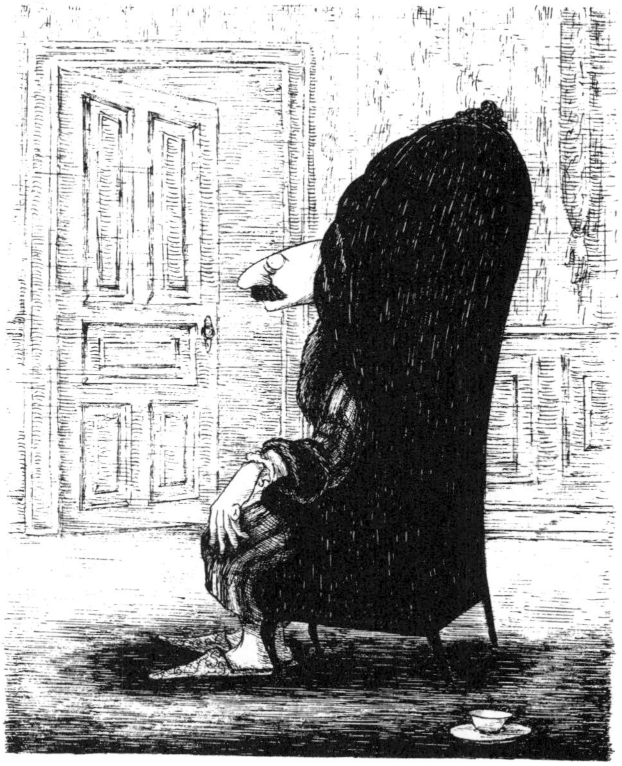

Some weeks later, with pen, ink, scissors, paste, a decanter of sherry, and a vast reluctance, Mr Earbrass begins to revise *TUH*. This means, first, transposing passages, or reversing the order of their paragraphs, or crumpling them up furiously and throwing them in the waste-basket. After that there is rewriting. This is worse than merely writing, because not only does he have to think up new things just the same, but at the same time try not to remember the old ones. Before Mr Earbrass is through, at least one third of *TUH* will bear no resemblance to its original state.

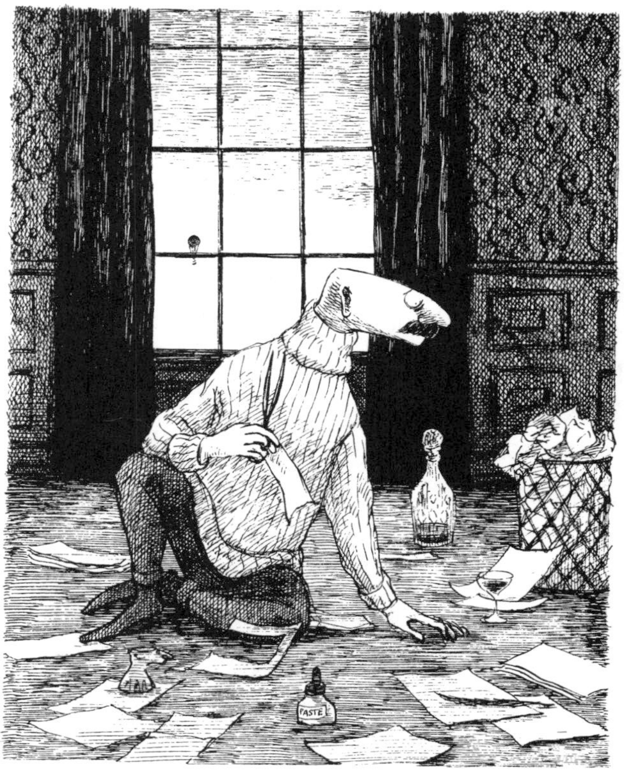
PASTE

Mr Earbrass sits on the opposite side of the study from his desk, gathering courage for the worst part of all in the undertaking of a novel, i.e., making a clean copy of the final version of the MS. Not only is it repulsive to the eye and hand, with its tattered edges, stains, rumpled patches, scratchings-out, and scribblings, but its contents are, by this time, boring to the point of madness. A freshly-filled inkwell, new pheasant-feather pens, and two reams of the most expensive cream laid paper are negligible inducements for embarking on such a loathsome proceeding.

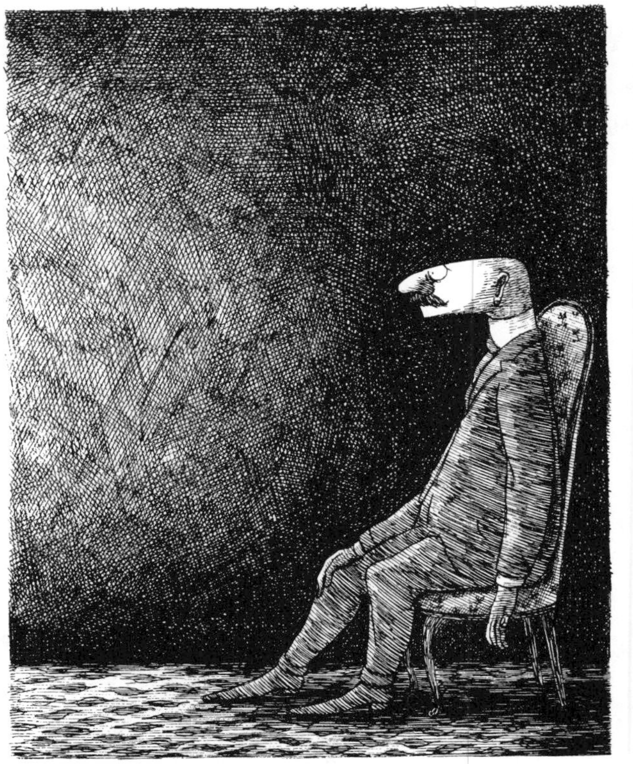

Holding *TUH* not very neatly done up in pink butcher's paper, which was all he could find in a last-minute search before leaving to catch his train for London, Mr Earbrass arrives at the offices of his publishers to deliver it. The stairs look oddly menacing, as though he might break a leg on one of them. Suddenly the whole thing strikes him as very silly, and he thinks he will go and drop his parcel off the Embankment and thus save everyone concerned a good deal of fuss.

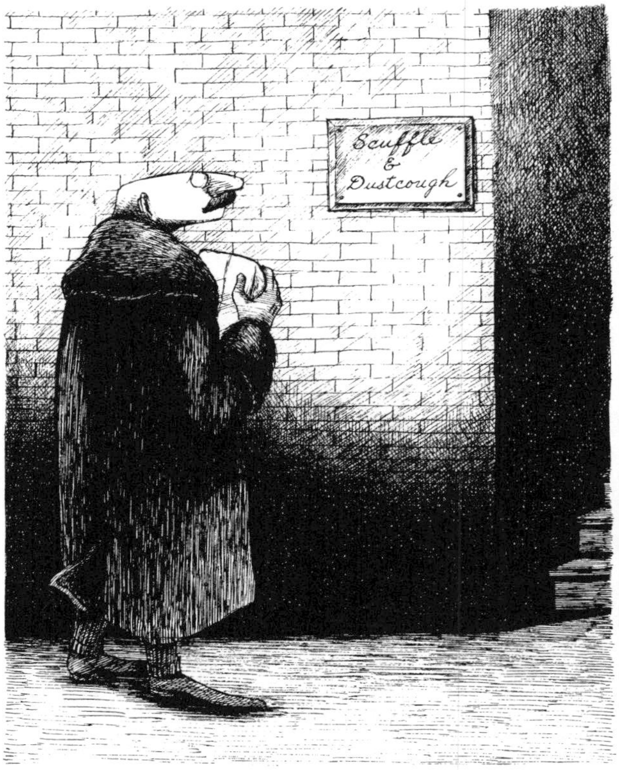
Scuffle & Dustcough

Mr Earbrass escaped from Messrs Scuffle and Dustcough, who were most anxious to go into all the ramifications of a scheme for having his novels translated into Urdu, and went to call on a distant cousin. The latter was planning to do the antique shops this afternoon, so Mr Earbrass agreed to join him. In the eighteenth shop they have visited, the cousin thinks he sees a rare sort of lustre jug, and Mr Earbrass irritatedly wonders why anyone should have had a fantod stuffed and put under a glass bell.

The night before returning home to Mortshire Mr Earbrass allows himself to be taken to a literary dinner in a private dining room of Le Trottoir Imbécile. Among his fellow-authors, few of whom he recognizes and none of whom he knows, are Lawk, Sangwidge, Ha'p'orth, Avuncular, and Lord Legbail. The unwell-looking gentleman wrapped in a greatcoat is an obscure essayist named Frowst. The talk deals with disappointing sales, inadequate publicity, worse than inadequate royalties, idiotic or criminal reviews, others' declining talent, and the unspeakable horror of the literary life.

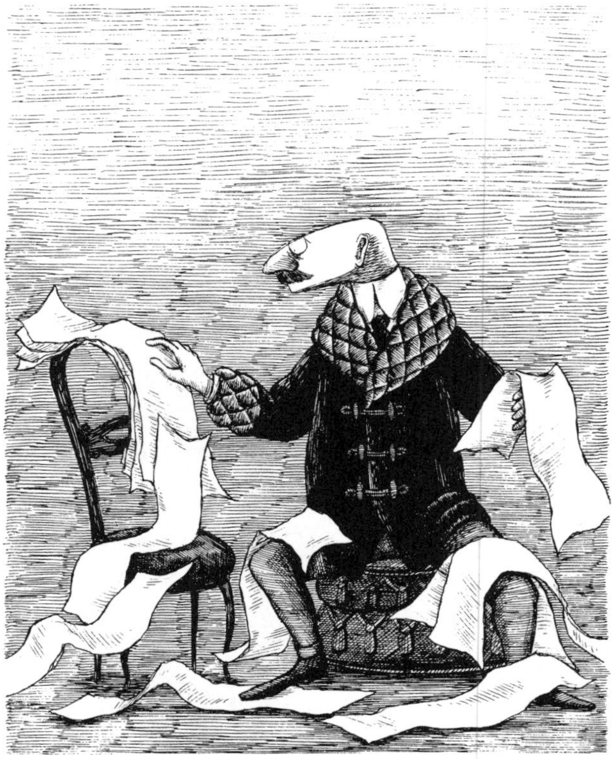

TUH is over so to speak, but far from done with. The galleys have arrived, and Mr Earbrass goes over them with mingled excitement and disgust. It all looks so different set up in type that at first he thought they had sent him the wrong ones by mistake. He is quite giddy from trying to physically control the sheets and at the same time keep the amount of absolutely necessary changes within the allowed pecuniary limits.

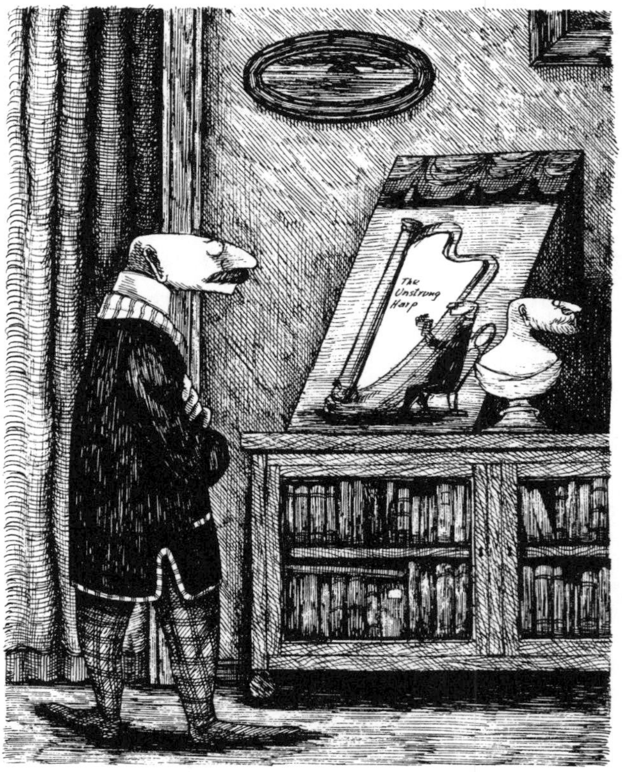
The Unstrung Harp

Mr Earbrass has received the sketch for the dust-wrapper of *TUH*. Even after staring at it continuously for twenty minutes, he really cannot believe it. Whatever were they thinking of? That drawing. Those colours. *Ugh*. On any book it would be ugly, vulgar, and illegible. On his book it would be these, and also disastrously wrong. Mr Earbrass looks forward to an exhilarating hour of conveying these sentiments to Scuffle and Dustcough.

Things contined to come, this time Mr Earbrass's six free copies of *TUH*. There are, alas, at least three times that number of people who expect to *receive one* of them. Buying the requisite number of additional copies does not happen to be the solution, as it would come out almost at once, and everyone would be very angry at his wanton distribution of them to just anyone, and write him little notes of thanks ending with the remark that *TUH* seems rather down from *your usual* level of polish but then *you* were probably in a hurry for the money. If it didn't come out, the list would be three times larger for his next book.

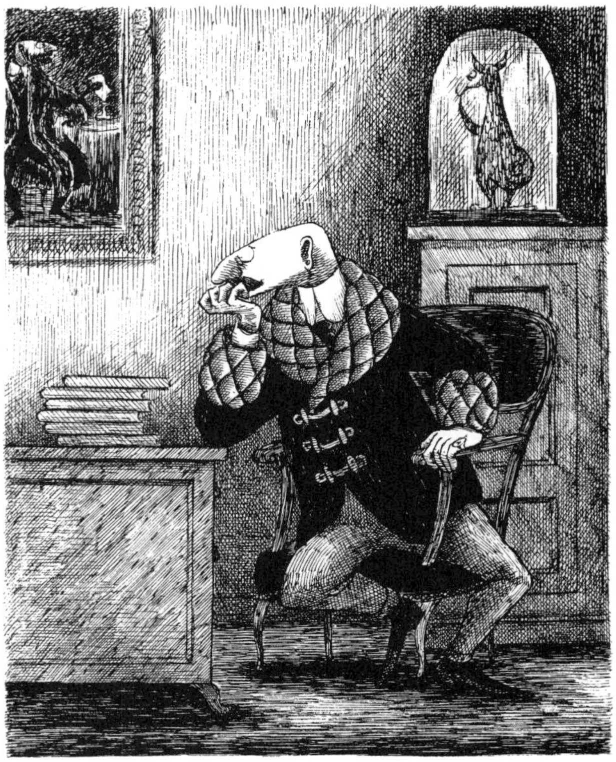

To-day *TUH* is published, and Mr Earbrass has come into Nether Millstone to do some errands which could not be put off any longer. He has been uncharacteristically thorough about doing them, and it is late afternoon before he pauses in front of a bookseller's window on the way back to his car. Having made certain, out of the corner of his eye, a copy of *TUH* was in it, he is carefully reading the title of every other book there in a state of extreme and pointless embarrassment.

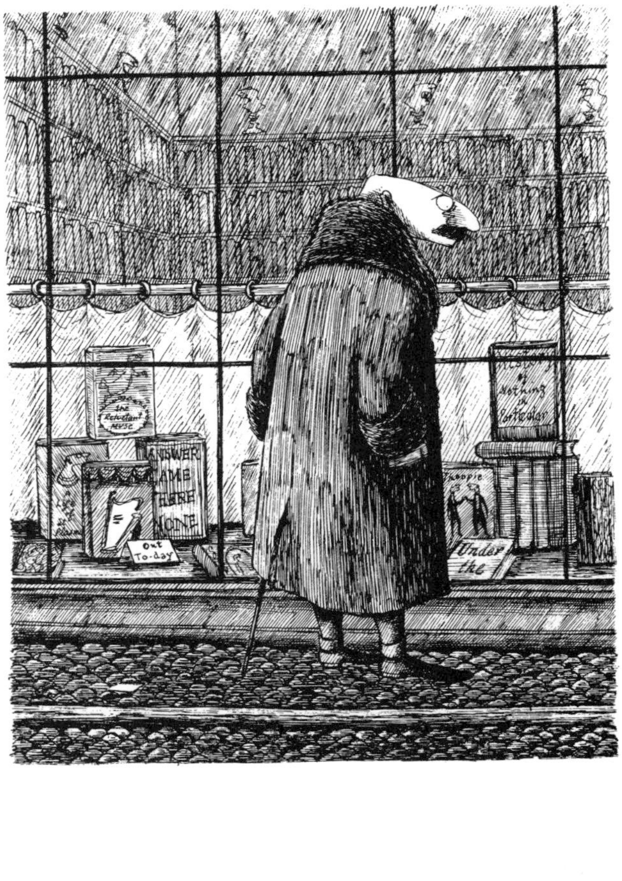
the Reluctant Muse
ANSWER
Out To-day
of Nothing in Particular
Under the

Scuffle and Dustcough have thoughtfully, if gratuitously, sent all the papers with reviews in them. They make a gratifyingly large heap. Mr Earbrass refuses to be intimidated into rushing through them, but he is having a certain amount of difficulty in concentrating on, or, rather, making any sense whatever out of, *A Compendium of the Minor Heresies of the Twelfth Century in Asia Minor*. He has been meaning to finish it ever since he began it two years and seven months before, at which time he bogged down on page 33.

At an afternoon forgathering at the Vicarage vaguely in Mr Earbrass's honor, where he has been busy handing round cups of tea, he is brought up short by Col Knout, M.F.H. of the Blathering Hunt. He demands to know just what Mr Earbrass was 'getting at' in the last scene of Chapter XIV. Mr Earbrass is afraid he doesn't know what the Colonel is. Is what? Getting at himself. The Colonel snorts, Mr Earbrass sighs. This encounter, which will go on for some time and get nowhere, will leave Mr Earbrass feeling very weak indeed.

Mr Earbrass stands on the terrace at twilight. It is bleak; it is cold; and the virtue has gone out of everything. Words drift through his mind: *anguish turnips conjunctions illness defeat string parties no parties urns desuetude disaffection claws loss Trebizond napkins shame stones distance fever Antipodes mush glaciers incoherence labels miasma amputation tides deceit mourning elsewards* ...

Before he knew what he was doing, Mr Earbrass found he had every intention of spending a few weeks on the Continent. In a trance of efficiency, which could have surprised no-one more than himself, he made the complicated and maddening preparations for his departure in no time at all. Now, at dawn, he stands, quite numb with cold and trepidation, looking at the churning surface of the Channel. He assumes he will be horribly sick for hours and hours, but it doesn't matter. Though he is a person to whom things do not happen, perhaps they may when he is on the other side.

THE
LISTING ATTIC

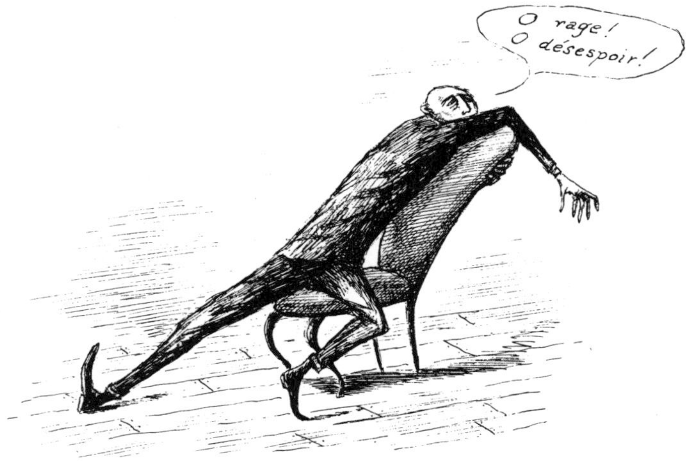
O rage!
O désespoir!

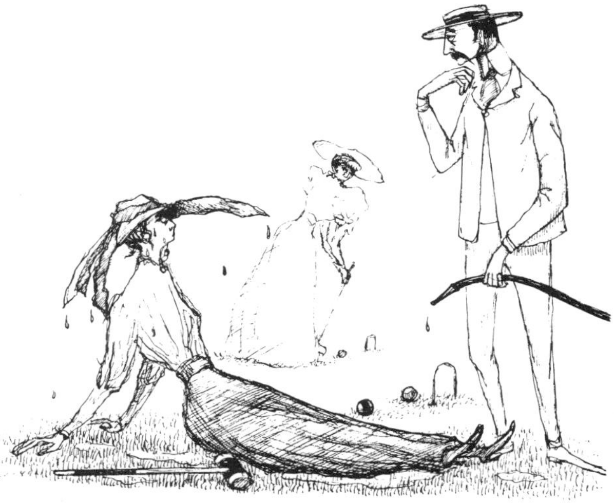

There was a young lady named Rose
Who fainted whenever she chose;
She did so one day
While playing croquet,
But was quickly revived with a hose.

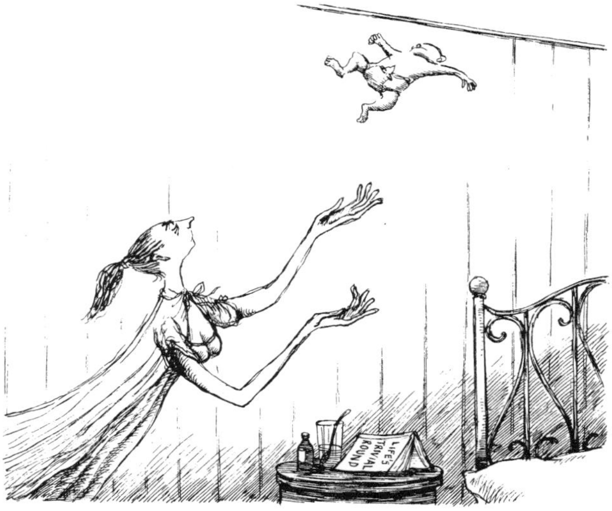
LIFE'S ETERNAL ROUND

A headstrong young woman in Ealing
Threw her two weeks' old child at the ceiling;
When quizzed why she did,
She replied, 'To be rid
Of a strange, overpowering feeling.'

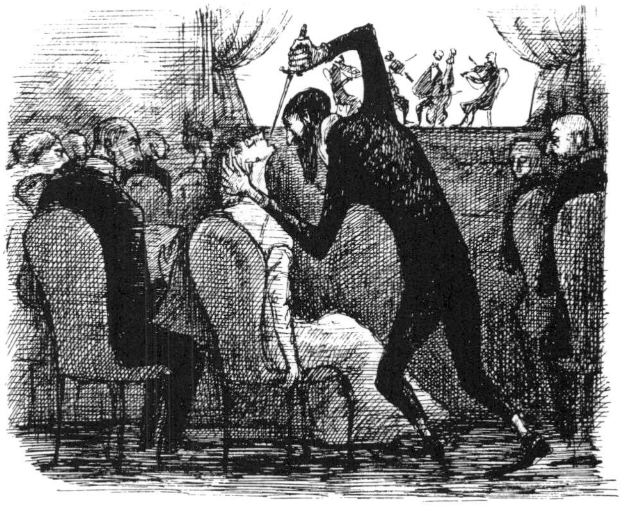

They had come in the fugue to the stretto
When a dark, bearded man from a ghetto
Slipped forward and grabbed
Her tresses and stabbed
Her to death with a rusty stiletto.

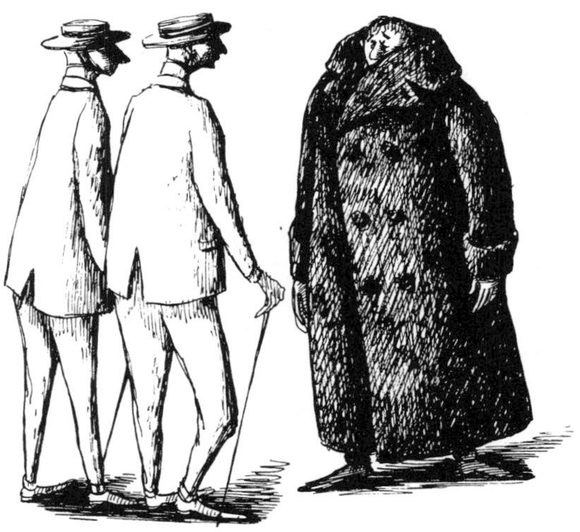

A certain young man, it was noted,
Went about in the heat thickly-coated;
He said, 'You may scoff,
But I shan't take it off;
Underneath I am horribly bloated.'

A lady was seized with intent
To revise her existence misspent,
 So she climbed up the dome
 Of St Peter's in Rome,
Where she stayed through the following Lent.

There was a young woman whose stammer
Was atrocious, and so was her grammar;
 But they were not improved
 When her husband was moved
To knock out her teeth with a hammer.

A dreary young bank clerk named Fennis
Wished to foster an aura of menace;
 To make people afraid
 He wore gloves of grey suede
And white footgear intended for tennis.

While his duchess lay practically dead,
The Duke of Daguerrodargue said:
 'Can it be this is all?
 How puny! How small!
Have destroyed this disgrace to my bed.'

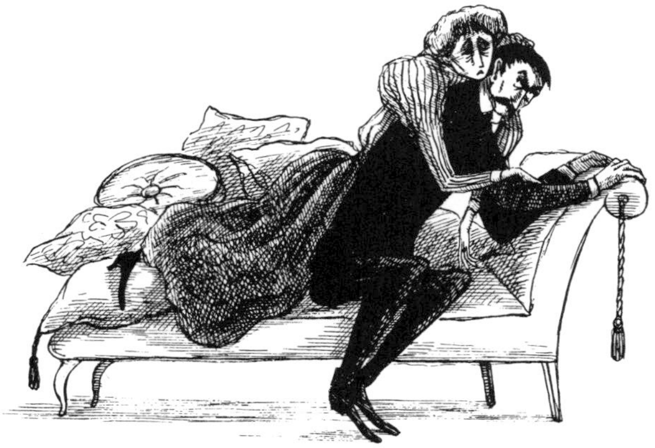

To a weepy young woman in Thrums
Her betrothed remarked, 'This is what comes
Of allowing your tears
To fall into my ears—
I think they have rotted the drums.'

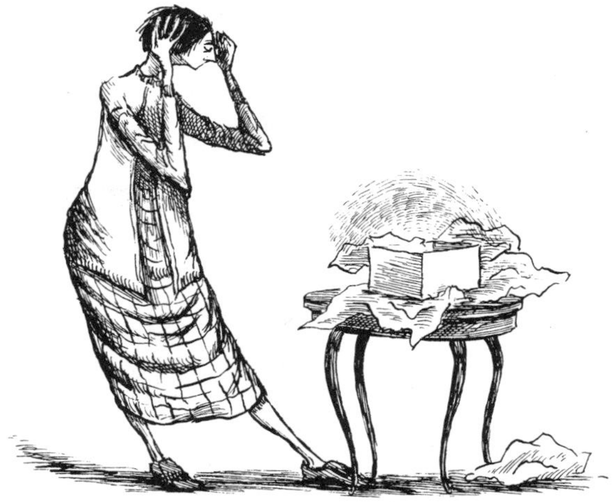

A gift was delivered to Laura
From a cousin who lived in Gomorrah;
Wrapped in tissue and crepe,
It was peeled, like a grape,
And emitted a pale, greenish aura.

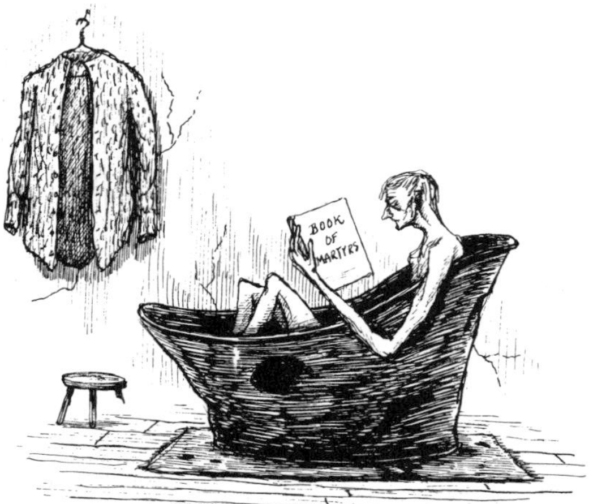
BOOK OF MARTYRS

A clerical student named Pryne
Through pain sought to reach the divine:
He wore a hair shirt,
Quite often ate dirt,
And bathed every Friday in brine.

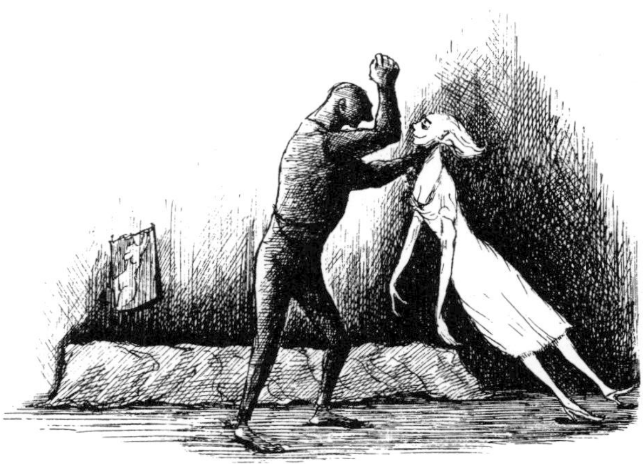

Il y a une jeune fille amoureuse
D'un homme qu'a une conduite honteuse;
Il la mene chaque soir
A son caveau noir
Et la bat avec plaintes crapuleuses.

'My trip? It was vile. Balaclava
I loathed. Etna was crawling with lava.
    The ship was all white
    But it creaked in the night,
And the band, they did not know la java.'

There was a young woman named Plunnery
Who rejoiced in the practice of gunnery,
    Till one day unobservant,
    She blew up a servant,
And was forced to retire to a nunnery.

A young man of acumen and daring,
Who'd amassed a great fortune in herring,
    Was left quite alone
    When it soon became known
That their use at his board was unsparing.

The partition of Vavasour Scowles
Was a sickener: they came on his bowels
    In a firkin; his brain
    Was found clogging a drain,
And his toes were inside of some towels.

As the breeches-buoy swung towards the rocks,
Its occupant cried, 'Save my socks!
   I could not bear the loss,
    For with scarlet silk floss
My mama has embroidered their clocks.'

An innocent maiden named Herridge
Was cruelly tricked into marriage;
   When she later found out
    What her spouse was about,
She threw herself under a carriage.

Les salons de la ville de Trieste
Sont vaseux, suraigus, et funestes;
   Parmi les grandes chaises
    On cause des malaises,
Des estropiéments, et des pestes.

Some Harvard men, stalwart and hairy,
Drank up several bottles of sherry;
   In the Yard around three
    They were shrieking with glee:
'Come on out, we are burning a fairy!'

An Edwardian father named Udgeon,
Whose offspring provoked him to dudgeon,
   Used on Saturday nights
   To turn down the lights,
And chase them around with a bludgeon.

The babe, with a cry brief and dismal,
Fell into the water baptismal;
   Ere they'd gathered its plight,
   It had sunk out of sight,
For the depth of the font was **abysmal**.

A lady both callous and brash
Met a man with a vast black moustache;
   She cried, 'Shave it, O do!
   And I'll put it with glue
On my hat as a sort of panache.'

A guest in a household quite charmless
Was informed its eccentric was harmless:
   'If you're caught unawares
   At the head of the stairs,
Just remember, he's eyeless and armless.'

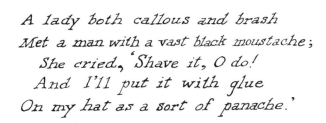

A beetling young woman named Pridgets
Had a violent abhorrence of midgets;
   Off the end of a wharf
   She once pushed a dwarf
Whose truncation reduced her to fidgets.

A lady born under a curse
Used to drive forth each day in a hearse;
   From the back she would wail
   Through a thickness of veil:
'Things do not get better, but worse.'

Each night Father fills me with dread
When he sits on the foot of my bed;
   I'd not mind that he speaks
   In gibbers and squeaks,
But for seventeen years he's been dead.

There was a young curate whose brain
Was deranged from the use of cocaine;
   He lured a small child
   To a copse dark and wild,
Where he beat it to death with his cane.

A young man grew increasingly peaky
In a house where the hinges were squeaky,
   The ferns curled up brown,
   The ceilings flaked down,
And all of the faucets were leaky.

The first child of a Mrs Keats-Shelley
Came to light with its face in its belly;
   Her second was born
   With a hump and a horn,
And her third was as shapeless as jelly.

There was a young woman named Ells
Who was subject to curious spells
   When got up very oddly,
   She'd cry out things ungodly
By the palms in expensive hotels.

At whist drives and strawberry teas
Fan would giggle and show off her knees;
   But when she was alone
   She'd drink eau de cologne,
And weep from a sense of unease.

There was a young sportsman named Peel
Who went for a trip on his wheel;
   He pedalled for days
    Through crepuscular haze,
And returned feeling somewhat unreal.

A timid young woman named Jane
Found parties a terrible strain;
   With movements uncertain
    She'd hide in a curtain
And make sounds like a rabbit in pain.

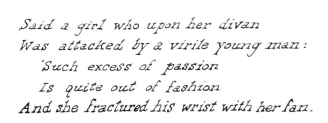

Said a girl who upon her divan
Was attacked by a virile young man:
   'Such excess of passion
    Is quite out of fashion'
And she fractured his wrist with her fan.

Un moine au milieu de la messe
S'éleva et cria en détresse:
   'La vie religieuse,
    C'est sale et affreuse'
Et se poignarda dans les fesses.

Augustus, for splashing his soup,
Was put for the night on the stoop;
   In the morning he'd not
   Repented a jot,
And next day he was dead of the croup.

A young lady who lived by the Usk
Subsisted each day on a rusk;
   She ate the first bite
   Before it was light,
And the last crumb sometime after dusk.

At the Villa Nemetia the sleepers
Are disturbed by a phantom in weepers;
   It beats all night long
   A dirge on a gong
As it staggers about in the creepers.

There was a young lady named Fleager
Who was terribly, terribly eager
   To be all the rage
   On the tragedy stage,
Though her talents were pitifully meagre.

A lady who signs herself 'Vexed'
Writes to say she believes she's been hexed:
  'I don't mind my shins
  Being stuck full of pins,
But I fear I am coming unsexed.'

A gentleman, otherwise meek,
Detested with passion the leek;
  When offered one out
  He dealt such a clout
To the maid, she was down for a week.

While travelling in farthest Tibet,
Lord Irongate found cause to regret
  The buttered-up tea,
  A pain in his knee,
And the frivolous tourists he met.

To his clubfooted child said Lord Stipple,
As he poured his post-prandial tipple,
  'Your mother's behaviour
  Gave pain to Our Saviour,
And that's why He made you a cripple.'

From the bathing machine came a din
As of jollification within;
    It was heard far and wide,
    And the incoming tide
Had a definite flavour of gin.

As tourists inspected the apse
An ominous series of raps
    Came from under the altar,
    Which caused some to falter
And others to shriek and collapse.

Pour guérir un accès de fièvre
Un jeune homme poursuivit un lièvre;
    Il le prit à son trou,
    Et fit faire un ragoût
Des entrailles et des pattes au genièvre.

A nurse motivated by spite
Tied her infantine charge to a kite;
    She launched it with ease
    On the afternoon breeze,
And watched till it flew out of sight.

There's a rather odd couple in Herts
Who are cousins (or so each asserts);
   Their sex is in doubt
   For they're never without
Their moustaches and long, trailing skirts.

The Dowager Duchess of Spout
Collapsed at the height of a rout;
   She found strength to say
   As they bore her away:
'I should never have taken the trout.'

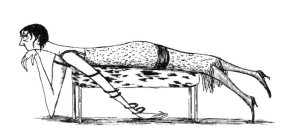

Said Francesca, 'My lack of volition
Is leading me straight to perdition;
   But I haven't the strength
   To go to the length
Of making an act of contrition.'

The sight of his guests filled Lord Cray
At breakfast with horrid dismay,
   So he launched off the spoons
   The pits from his prunes
At their heads as they neared the buffet.

An incautious young woman named Venn
Was seen with the wrong sort of men;
  She vanished one day,
  But the following May
Her legs were retrieved from a fen.

An indefatigable woman named Bavel
Had often occasion to travel;
  On the way she would sit
  And furiously knit,
And on the way back she'd unravel.

Having made a remark rather coarse,
A young lady was seized with remorse;
  She fled from the room,
  And later, a groom
Saw her rolling about in the gorse.

An old gentleman's crotchets and quibblings
Were a terrible trial to his siblings,
  But he was not removed
  Till one day it was proved
That the bell-ropes were damp with his dribblings.

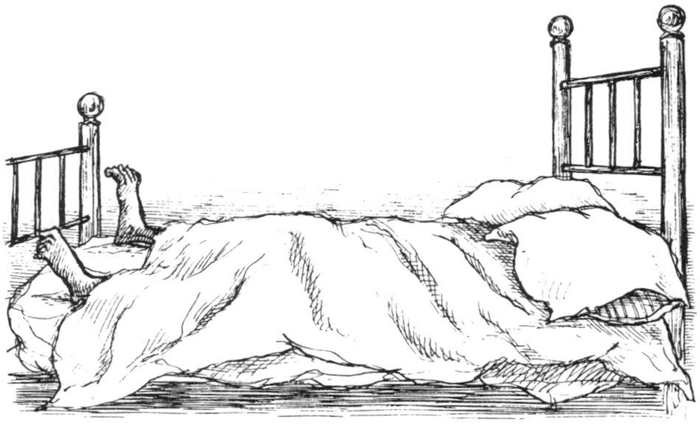

There was a young man, name of Fred,
Who spent every Thursday in bed;
He lay with his feet
Outside of the sheet,
And the pillows on top of his head.

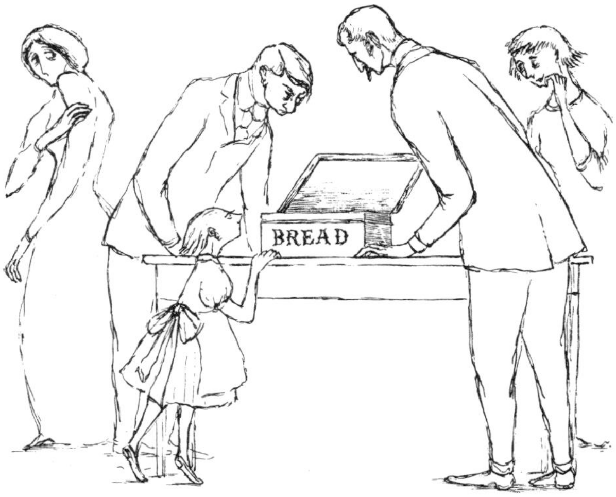
BREAD

From Number Nine, Penwiper Mews,
There is really abominable news:
They've discovered a head
In the box for the bread,
But nobody seems to know whose.

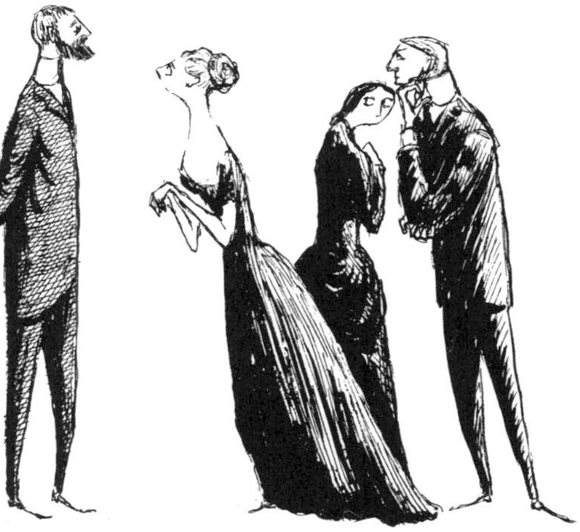

There was a young man who appeared
To his friends with a full growth of beard;
They at once said, 'Although
We can't say why it's so,
The effect is uncommonly weird.'

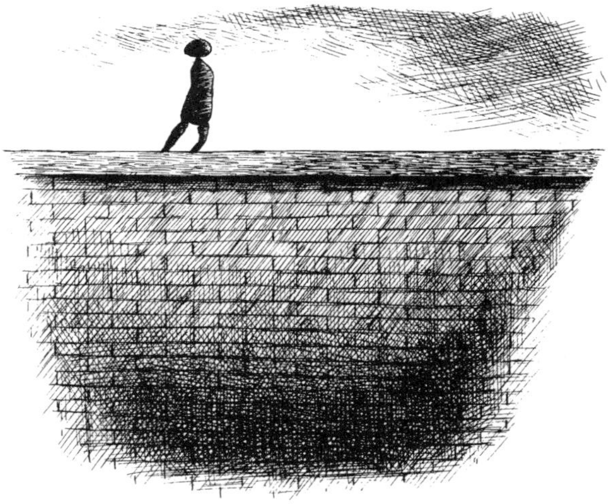

Ce Livre est dédié à Chagrin,
Qui fit un petit mannequin:
Sans bras et tout noir,
Il était affreux voir;
En effet, absolument la fin.

The Doubtful Guest

by Edward Gorey

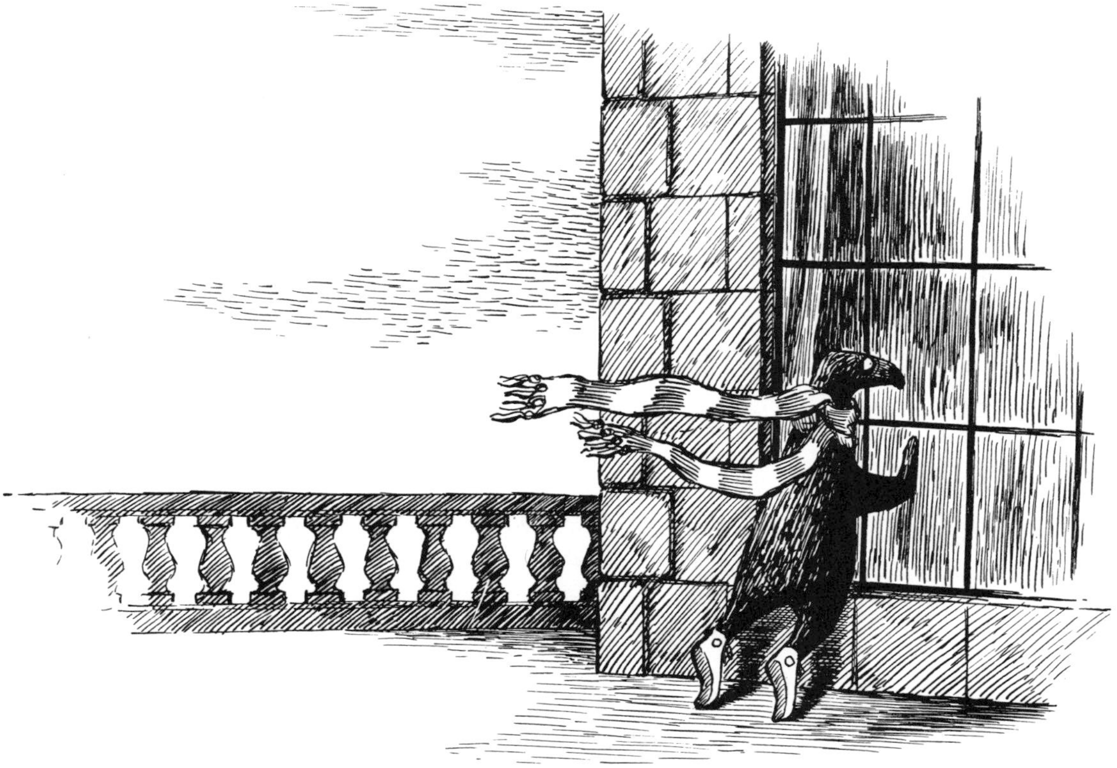

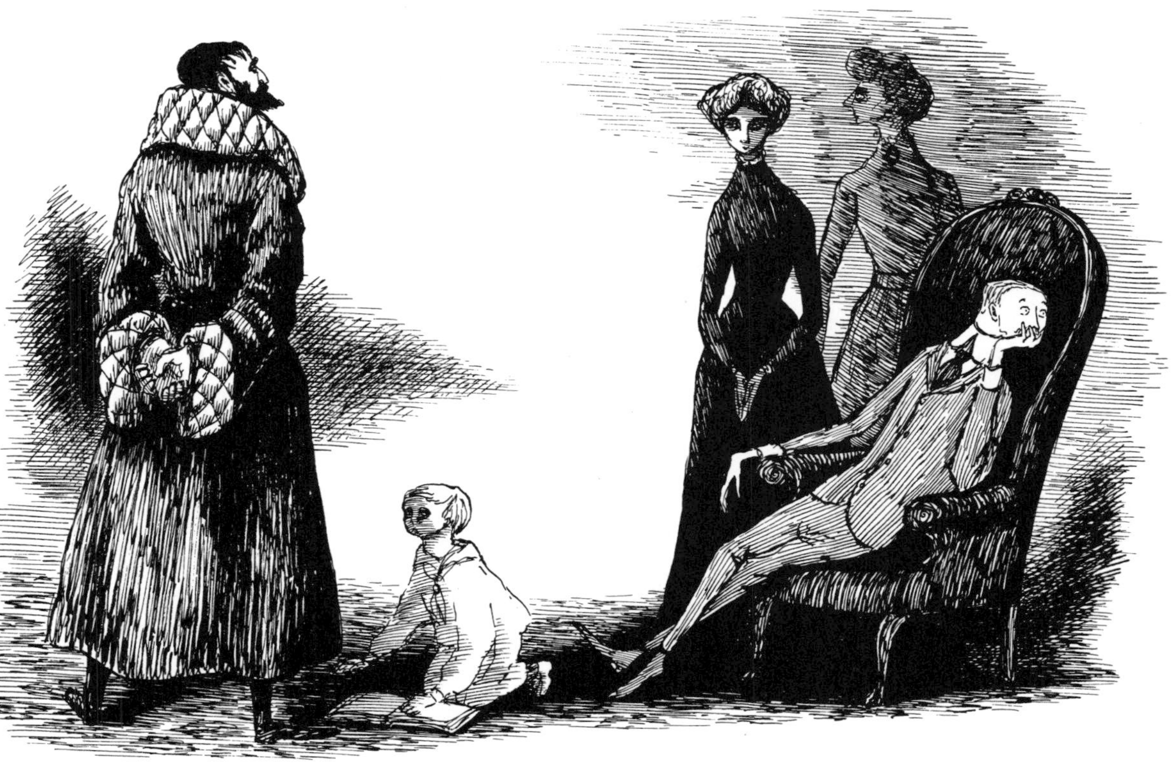

When they answered the bell on that wild winter night,
There was no one expected – and no one in sight.

Then they saw something standing on top of an urn,
Whose peculiar appearance gave them quite a turn.

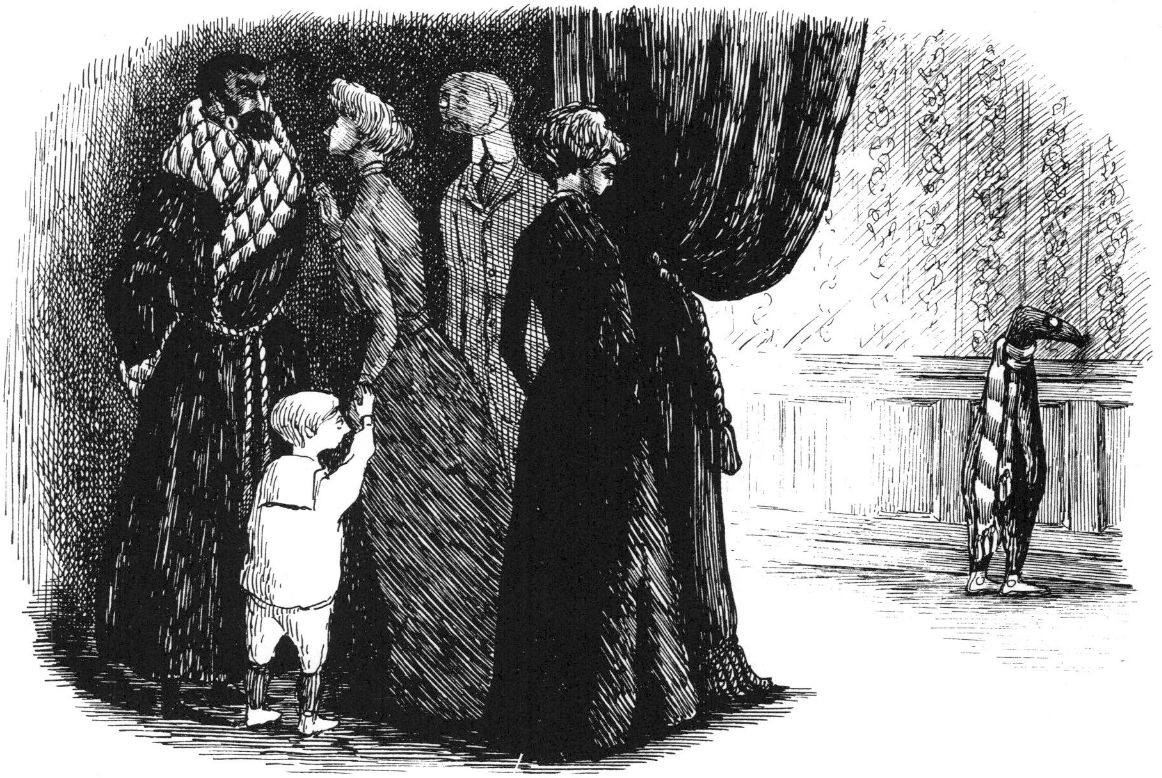

All at once it leapt down and ran into the hall,
Where it chose to remain with its nose to the wall.

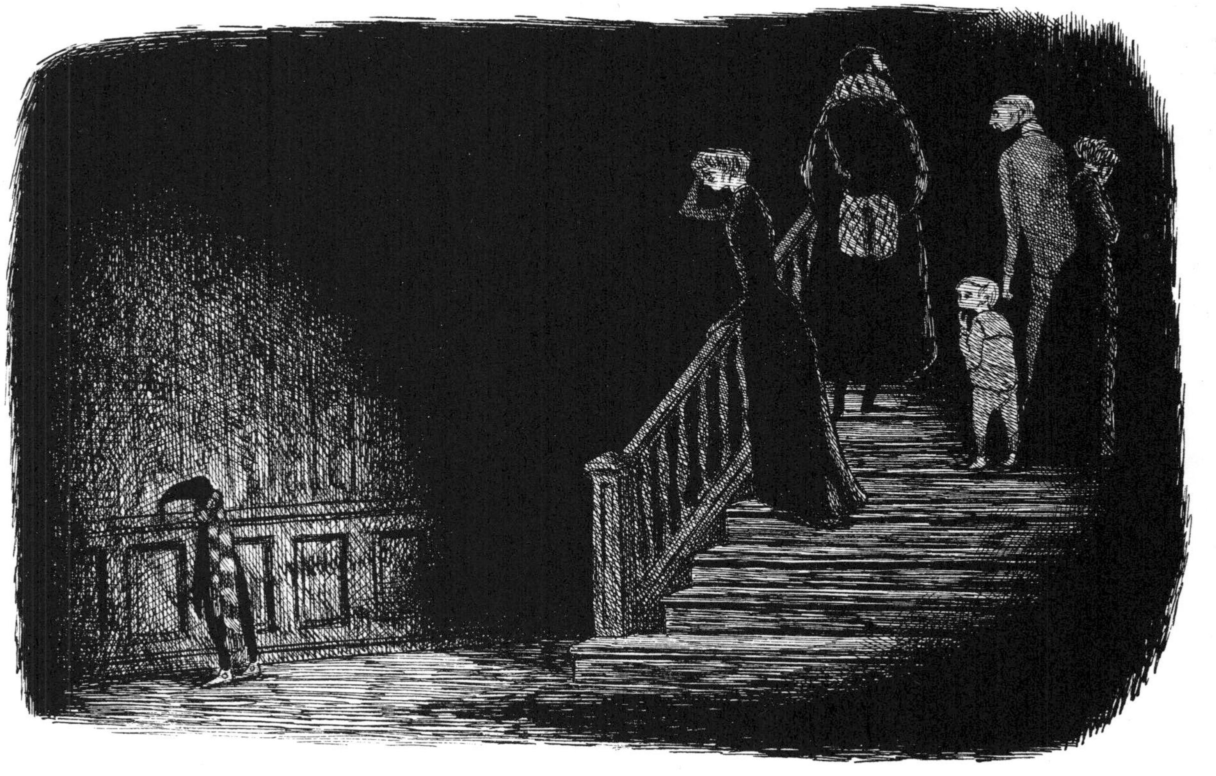

It was seemingly deaf to whatever they said,
So at last they stopped screaming, and went off to bed.

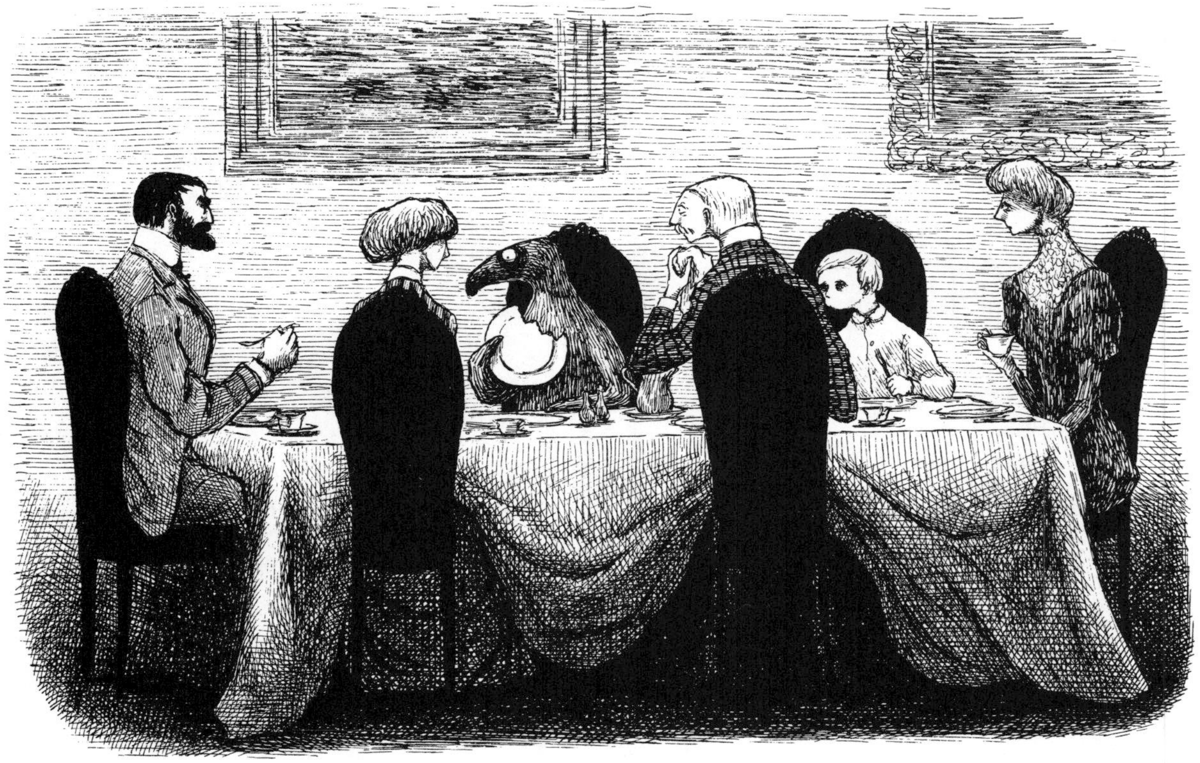

It joined them at breakfast and presently ate
All the syrup and toast, and a part of a plate.

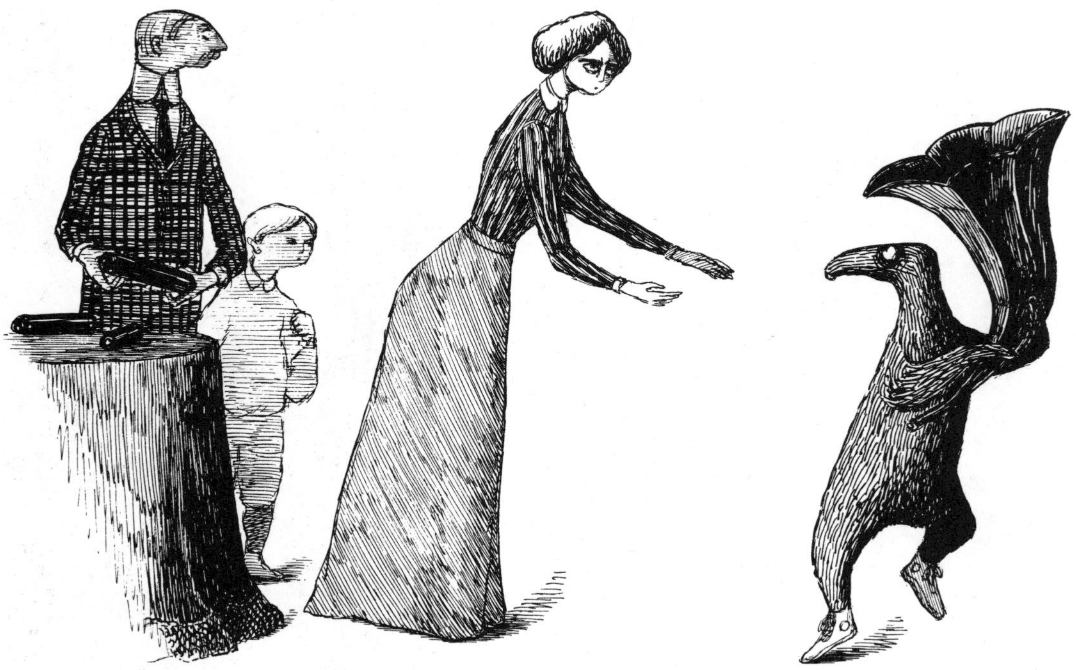

It wrenched off the horn from the new gramophone,
And could not be persuaded to leave it alone.

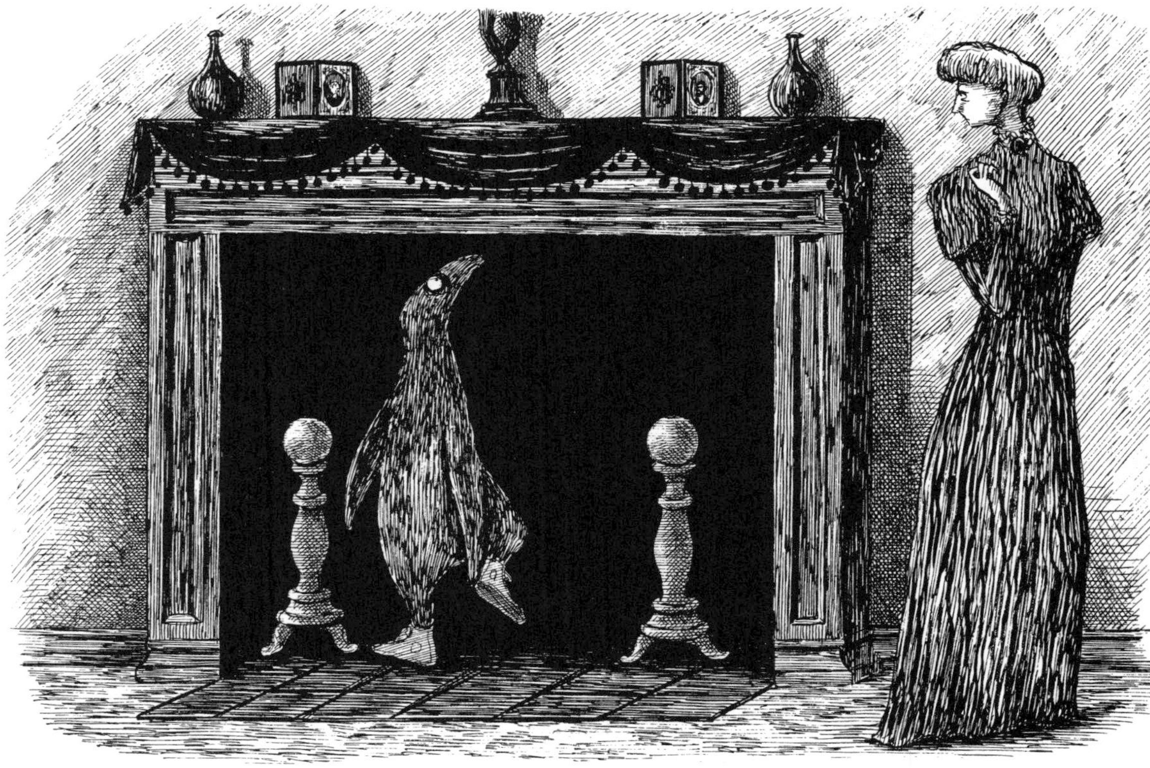

It betrayed a great liking for peering up flues,
And for peeling the soles of its white canvas shoes.

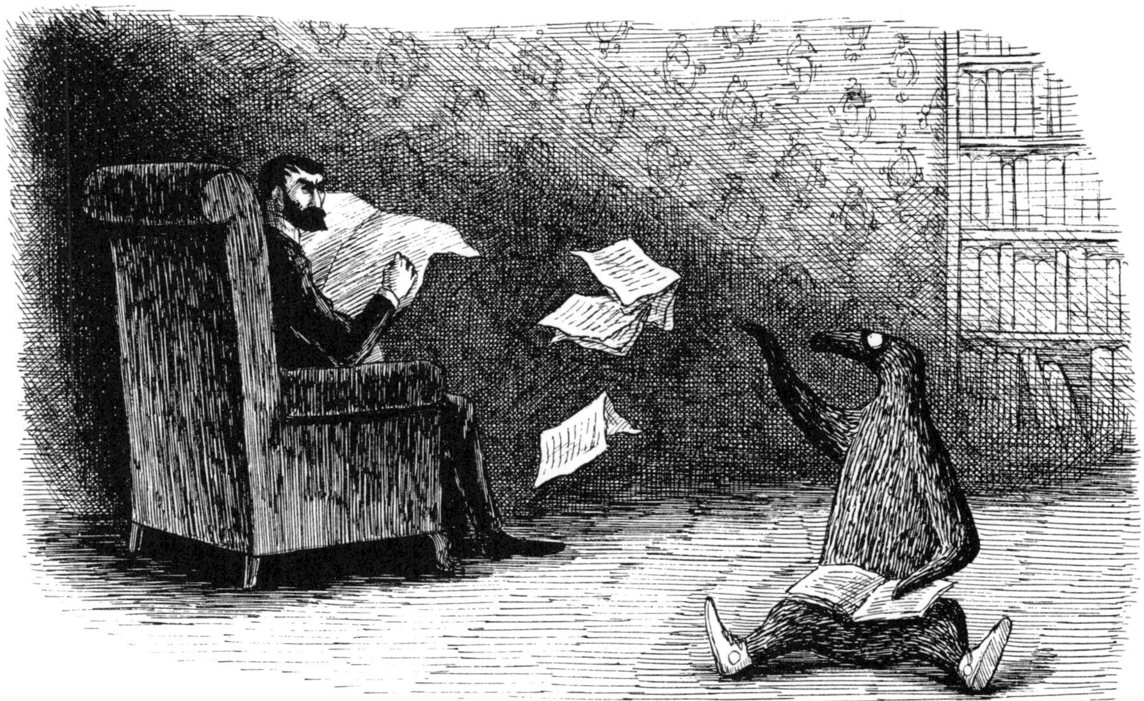

At times it would tear out whole chapters from books,
Or put roomfuls of pictures askew on their hooks.

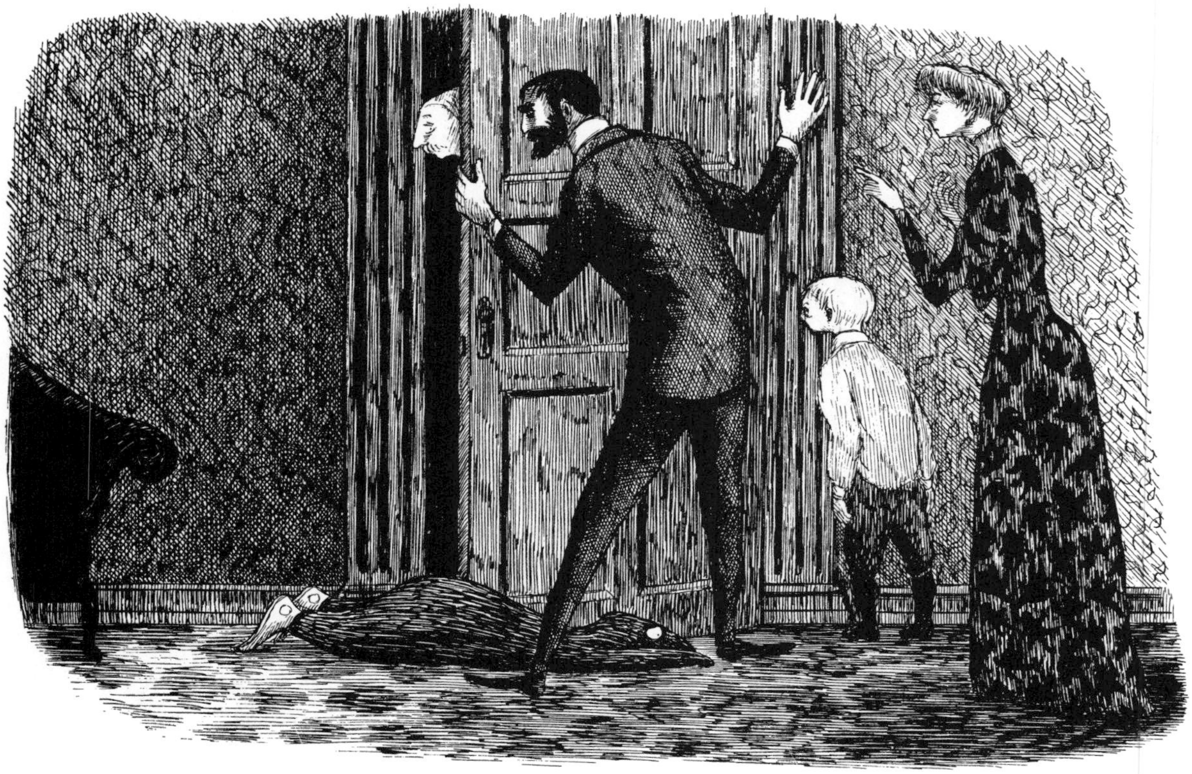

Every Sunday it brooded and lay on the floor,
Inconveniently close to the drawing-room door.

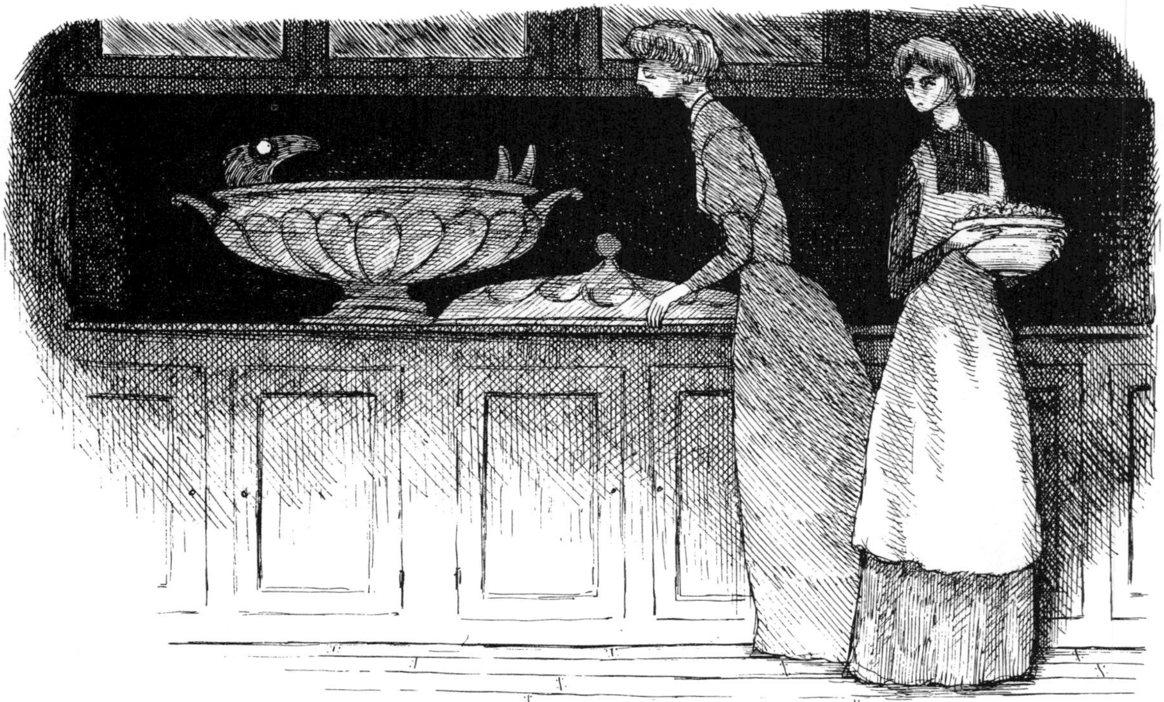

Now and then it would vanish for hours from the scene,
But alas, be discovered inside a tureen.

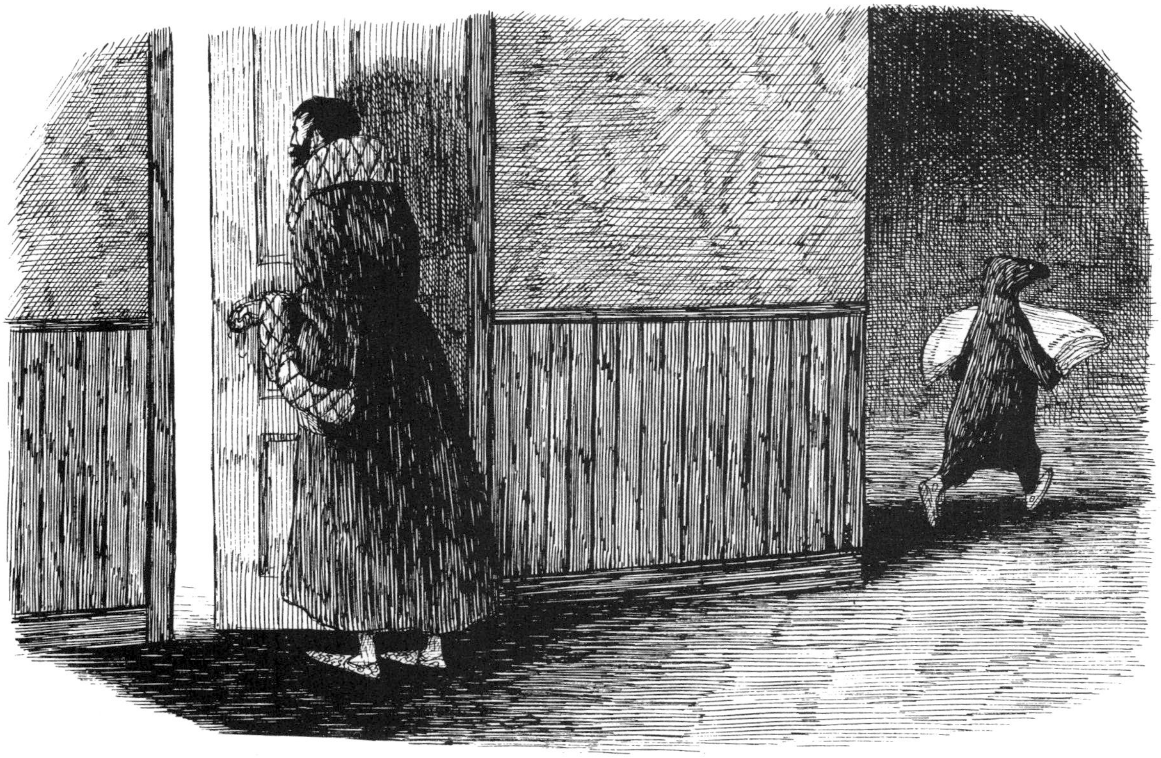

It was subject to fits of bewildering wrath,
During which it would hide all the towels from the bath.

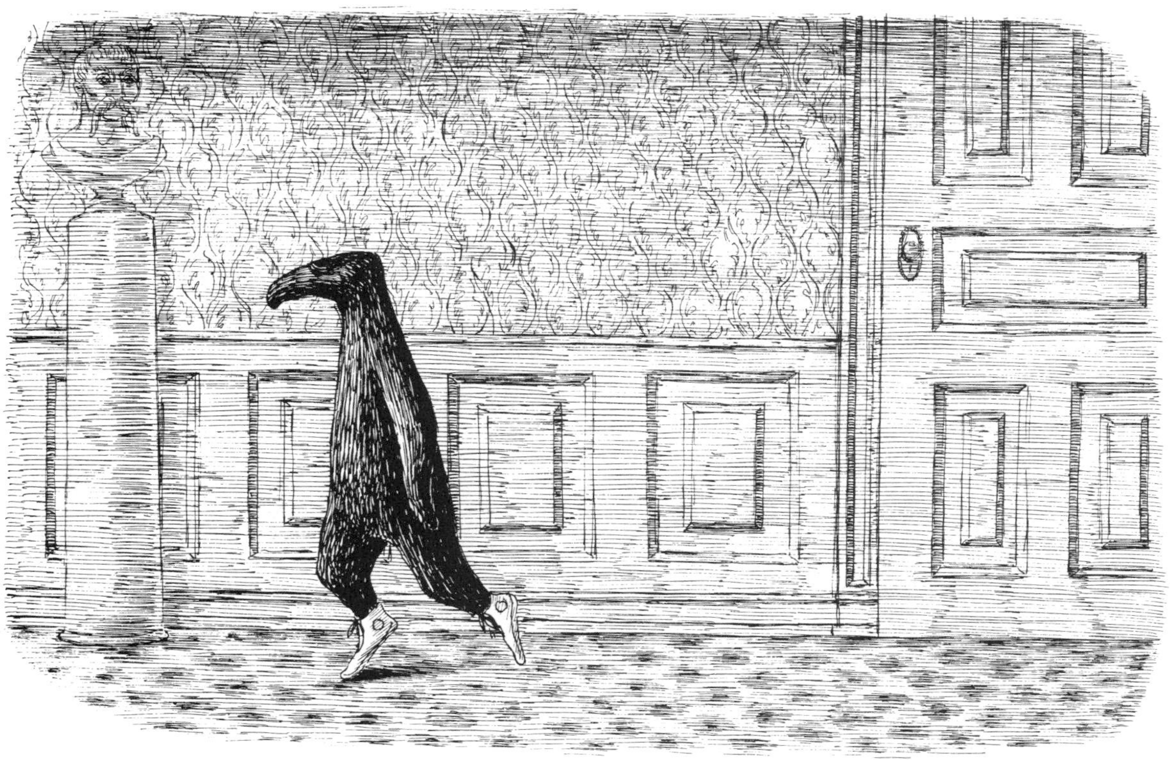

In the night through the house it would aimlessly creep,
In spite of the fact of its being asleep.

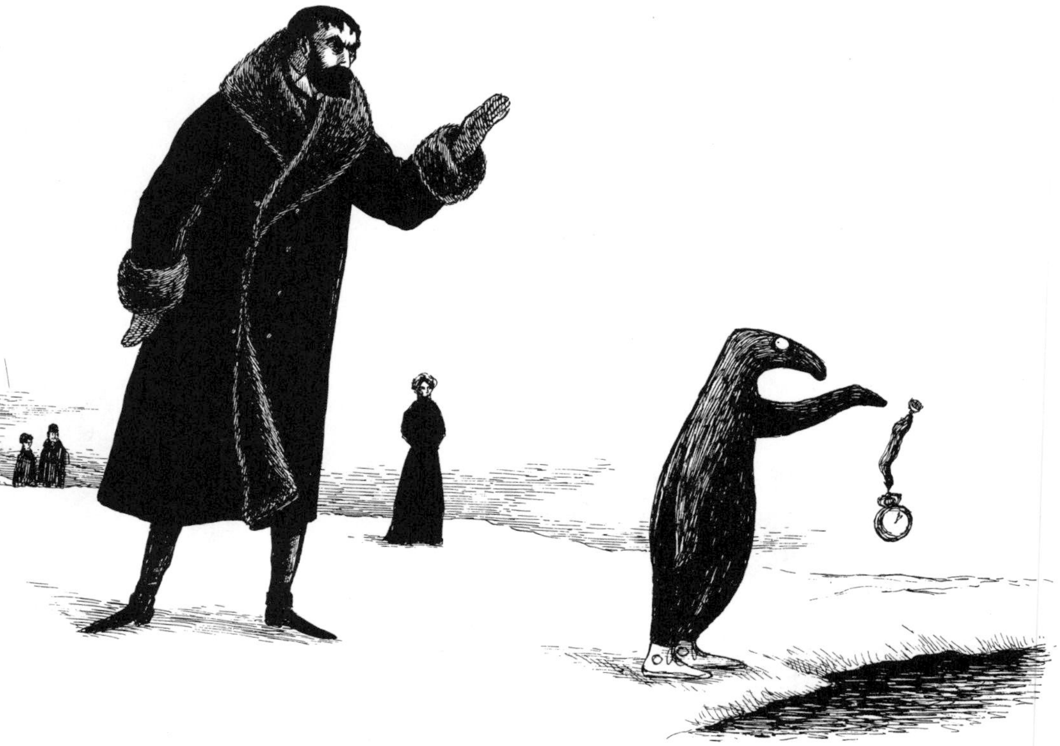

It would carry off objects of which it grew fond,
And protect them by dropping them into the pond.

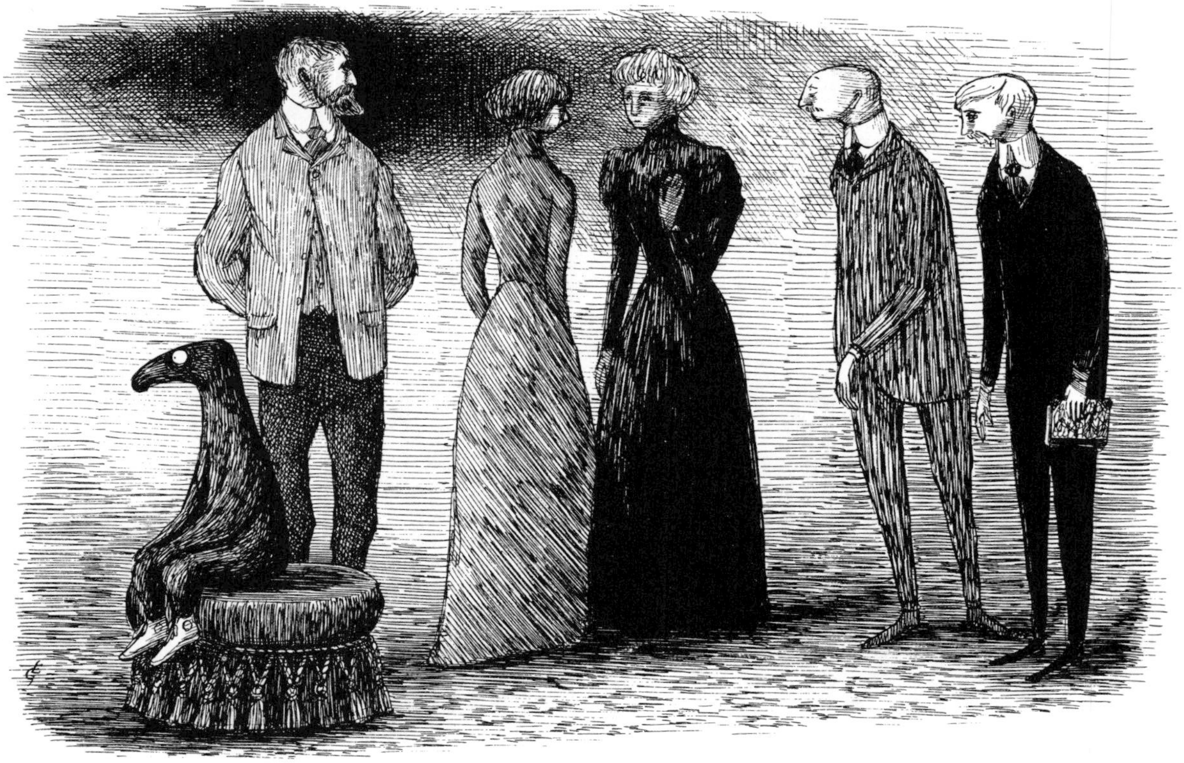

It came seventeen years ago – and to this day
It has shown no intention of going away.

THE OBJECT-LESSON

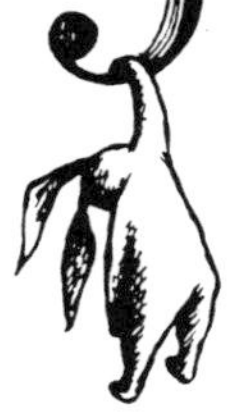

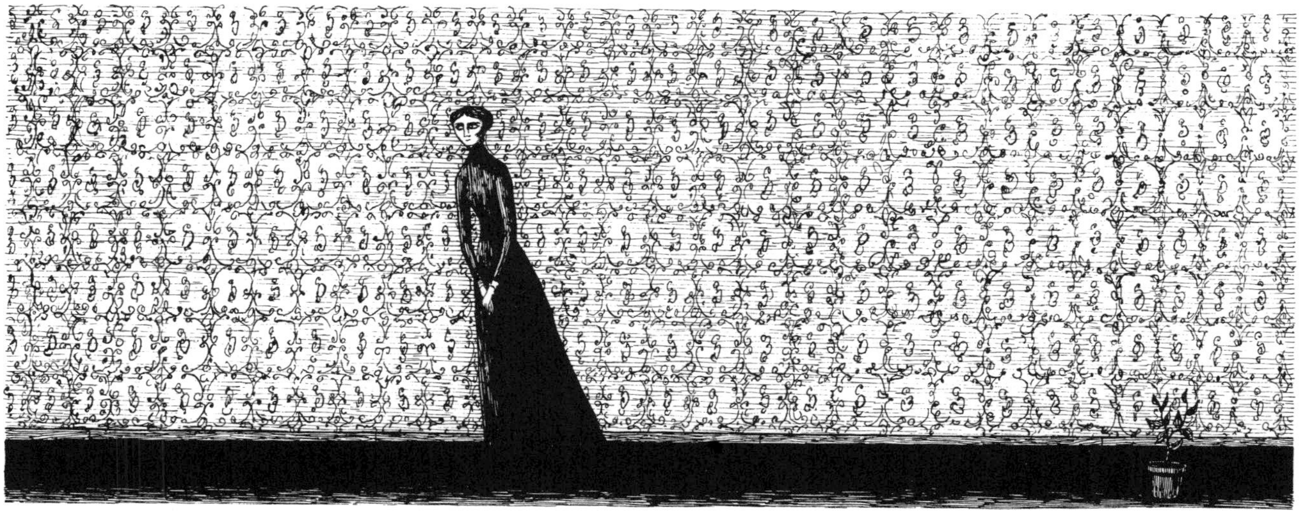

It was already Thursday,

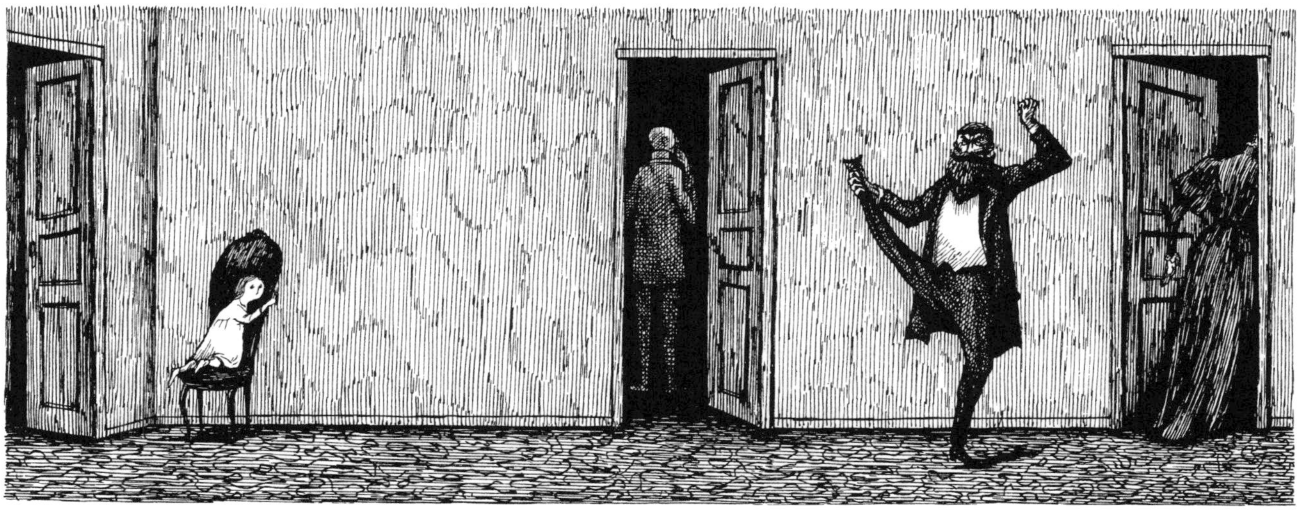

but his lordship's artificial limb could not be found;

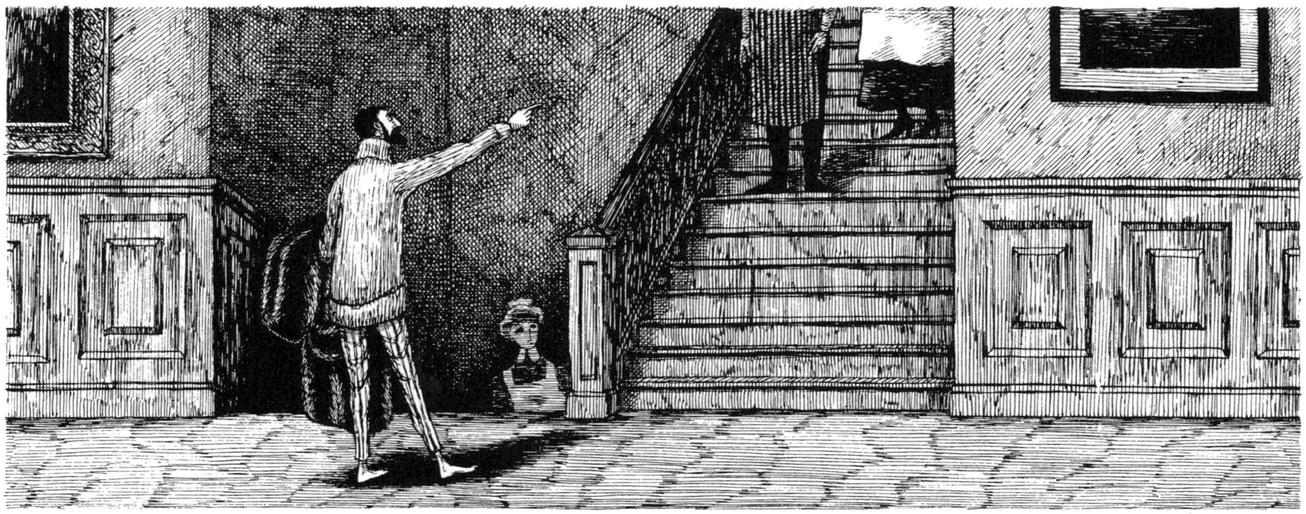

therefore, having directed the servants to fill the baths,

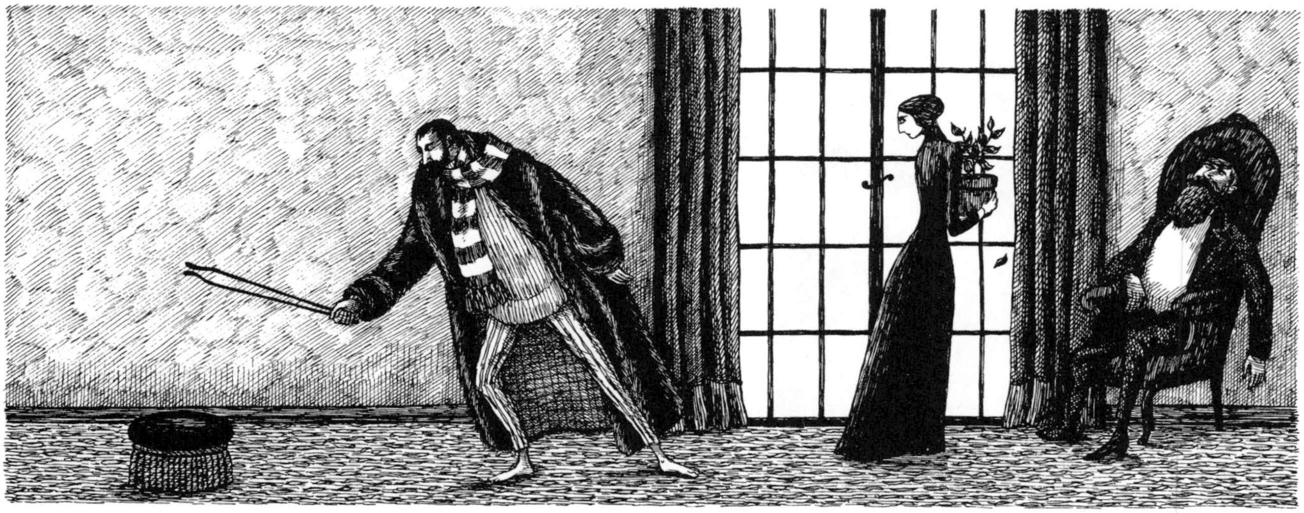

he seized the tongs

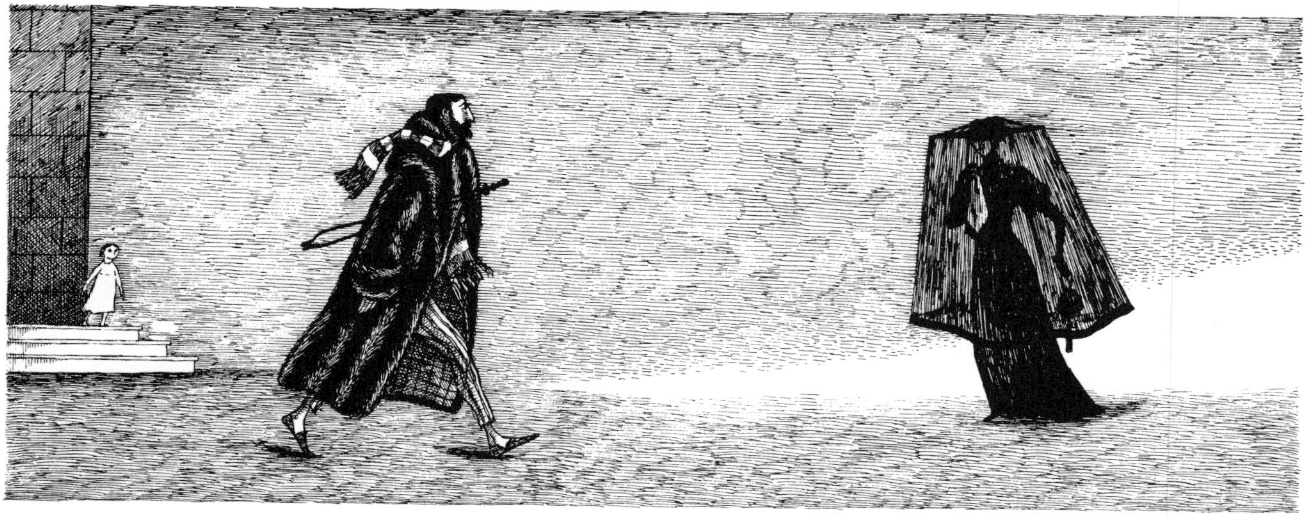

and set out at once for the edge of the lake,

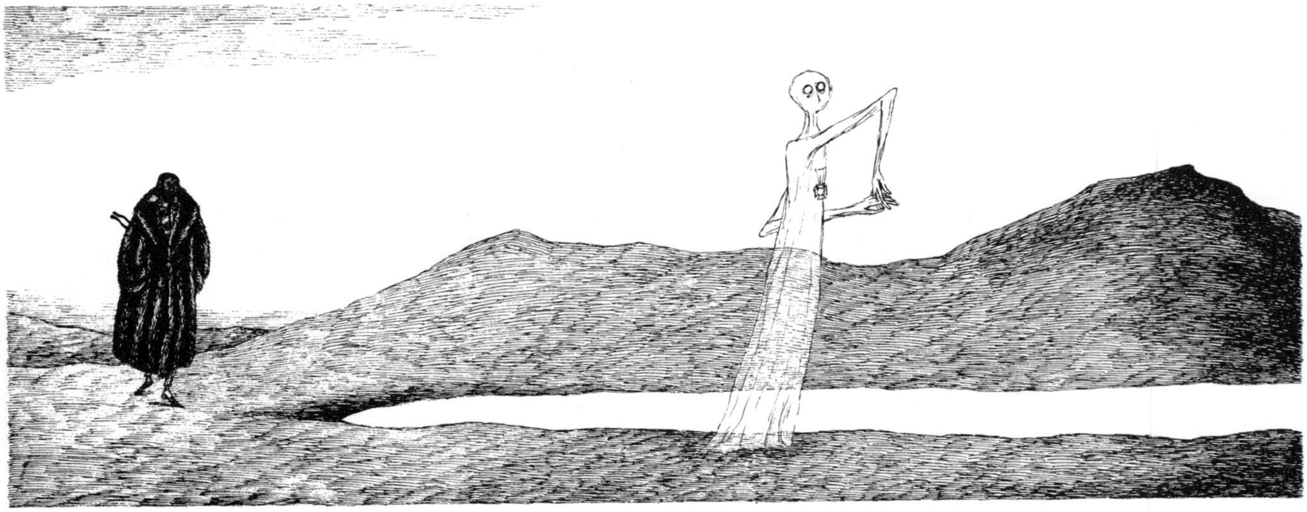

where the Throbblefoot Spectre still loitered in a distraught manner.

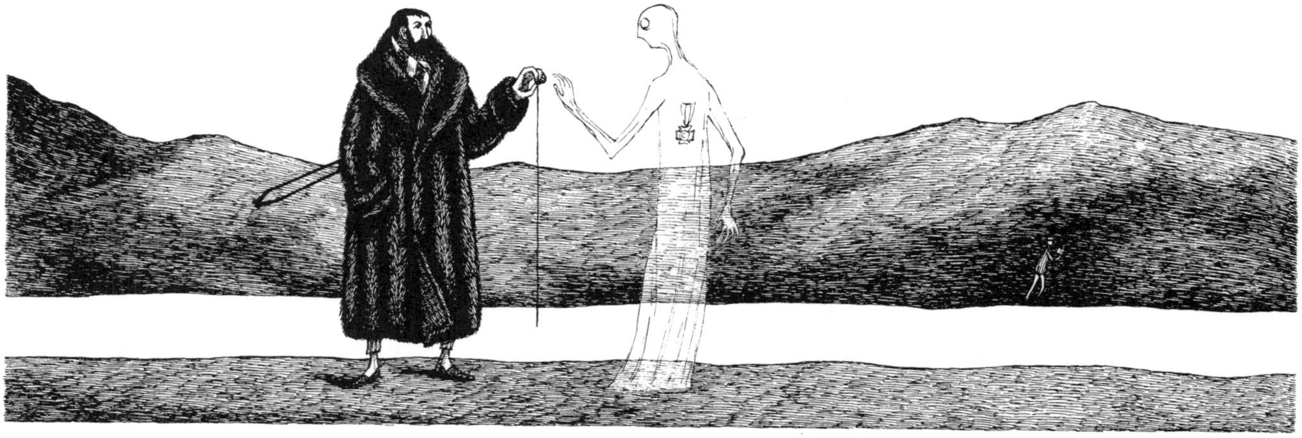

He presented it with a length of string

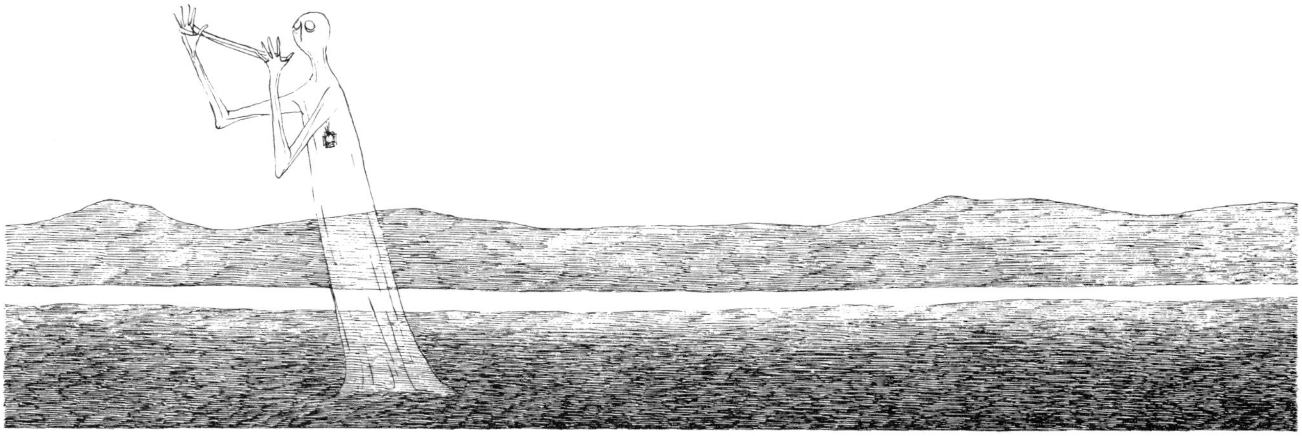

and passed on to the statue of Corrupted Endeavour

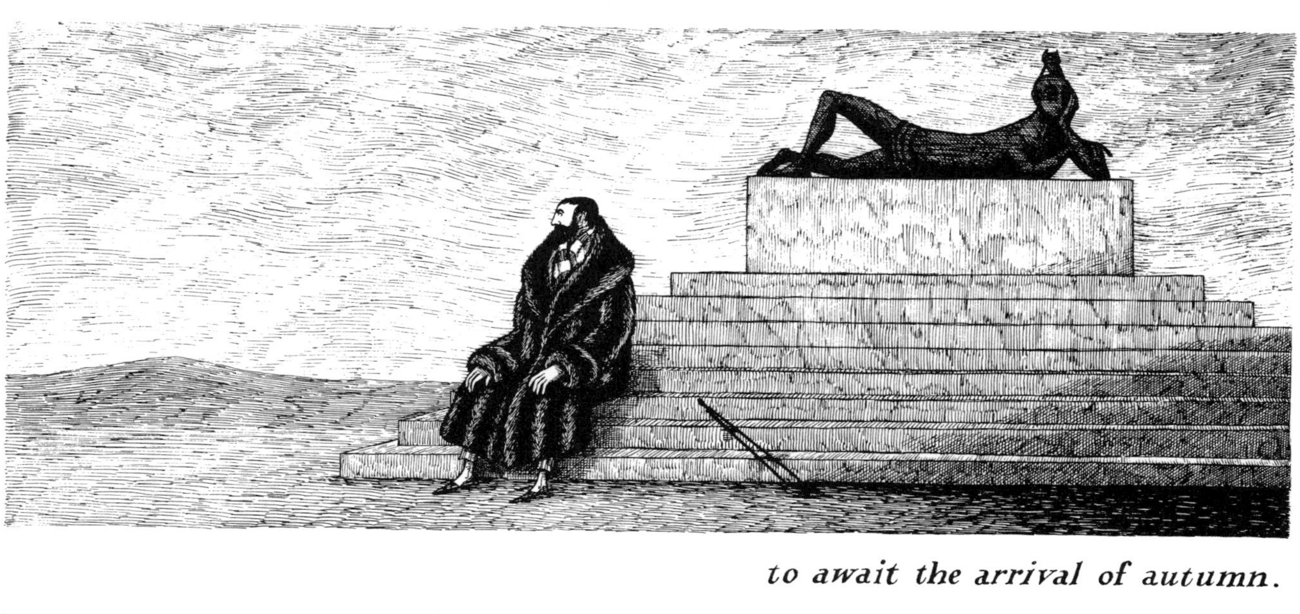

to await the arrival of autumn.

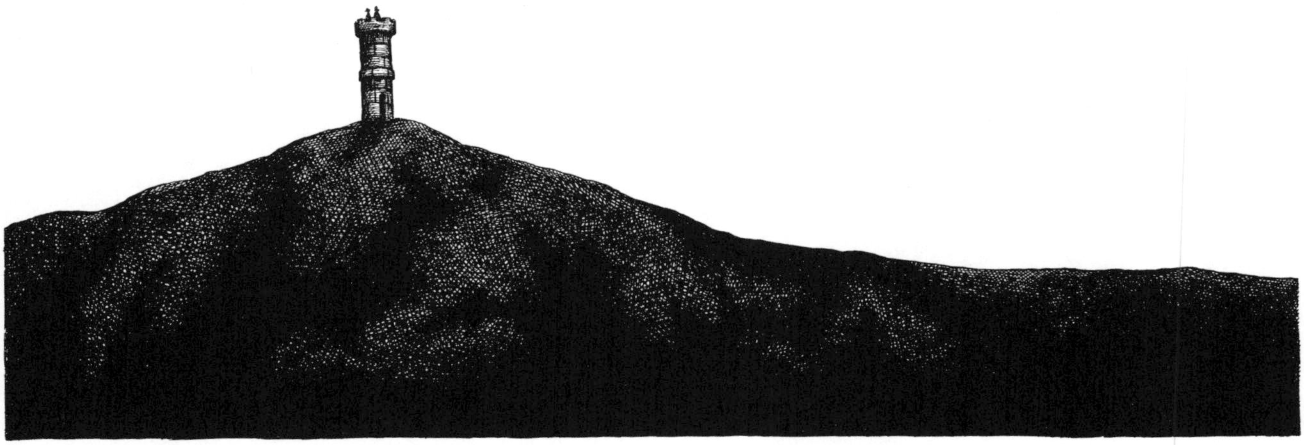

Meanwhile, on the tower,

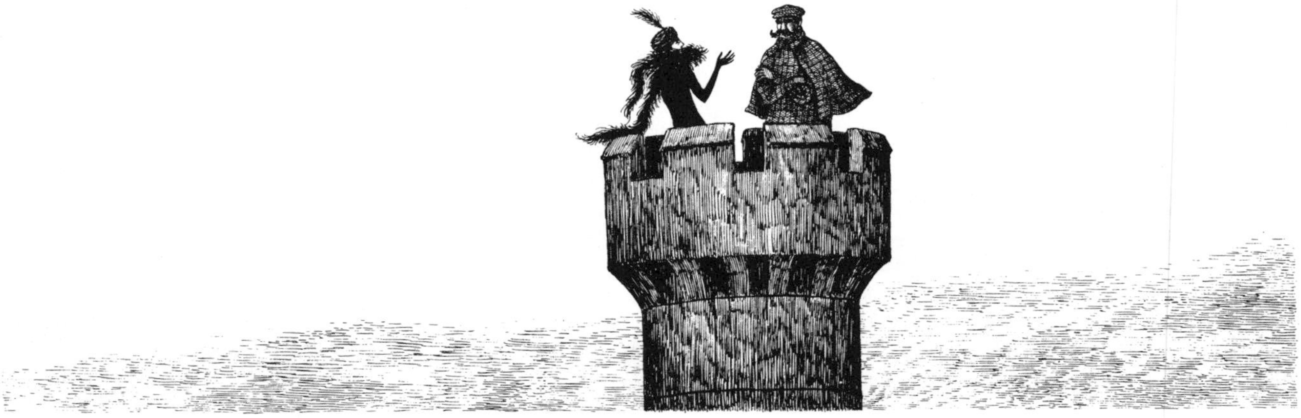

Madame O_____ in conversation with an erstwhile cousin

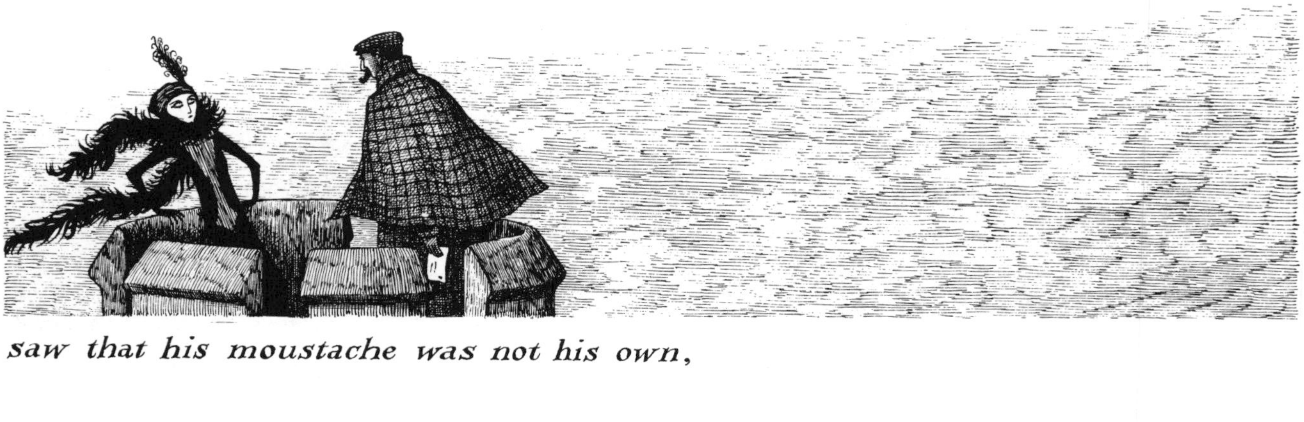

saw that his moustache was not his own,

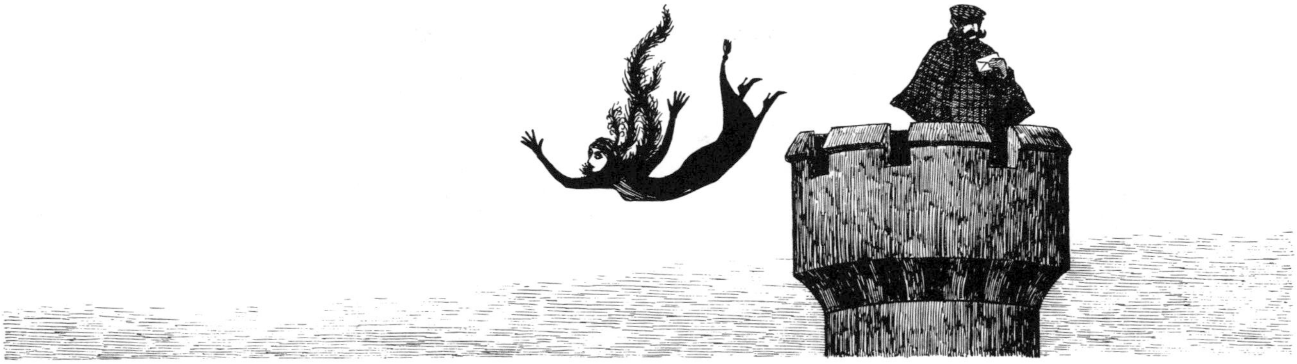

on which she flung herself over the parapet

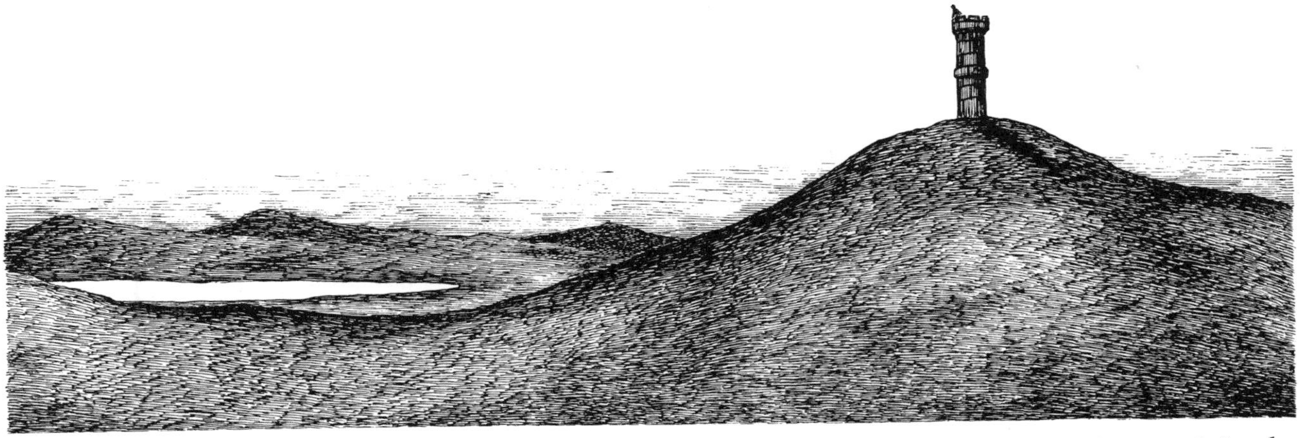

and surreptitiously vanished.

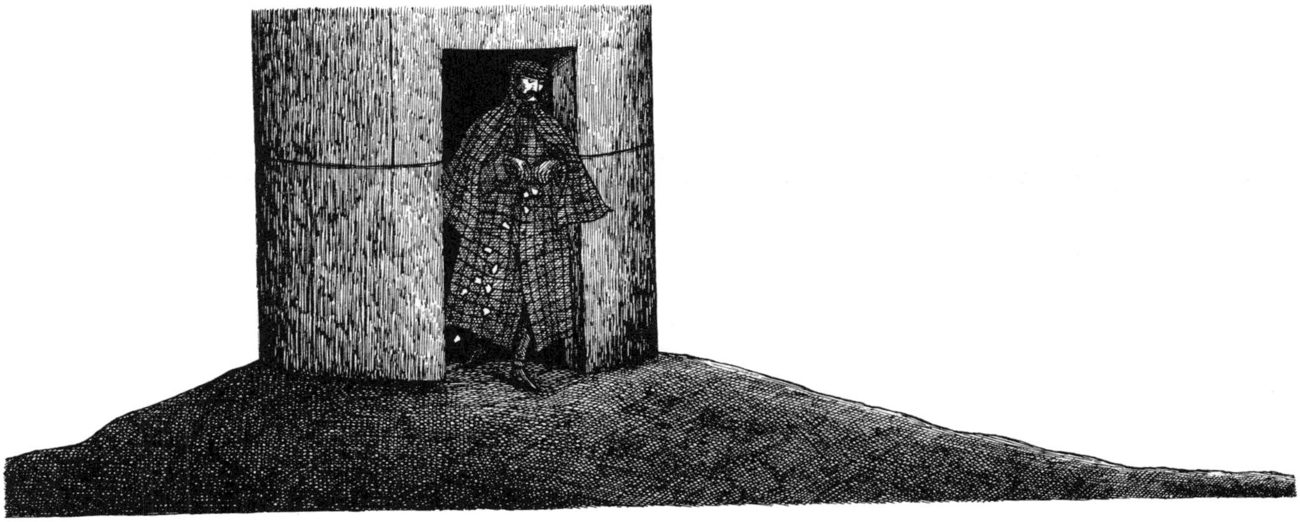

He descended, destroying the letter unread,

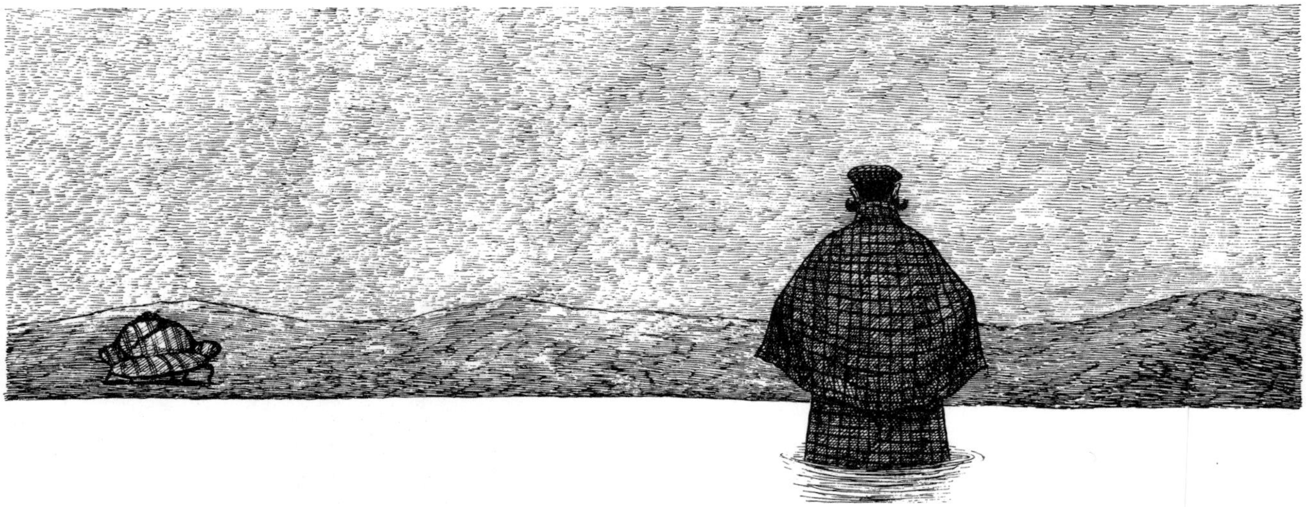

and stepped backwards into the water for a better view.

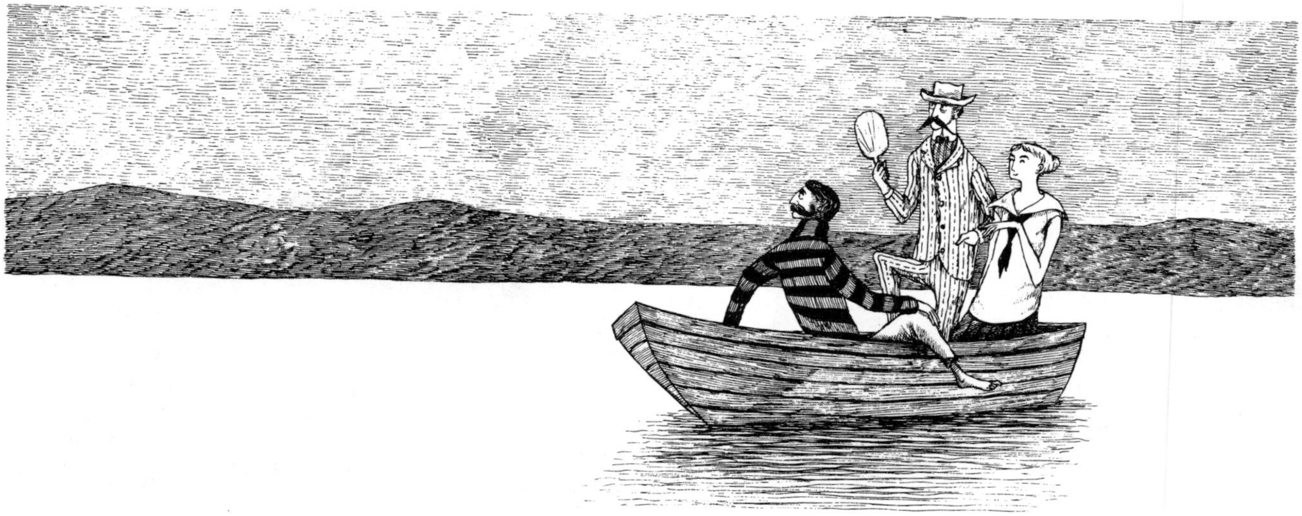

Heavens, how dashing! cried the people in the dinghy,

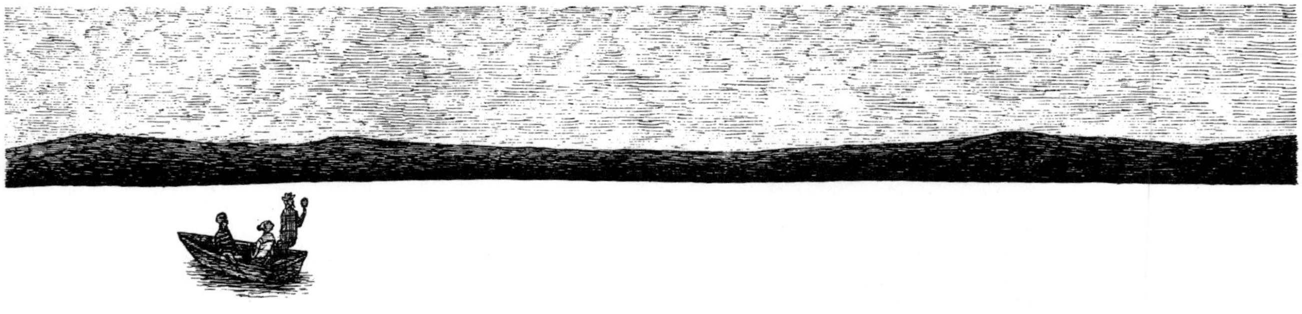

and Echo answered: Count the spoons!

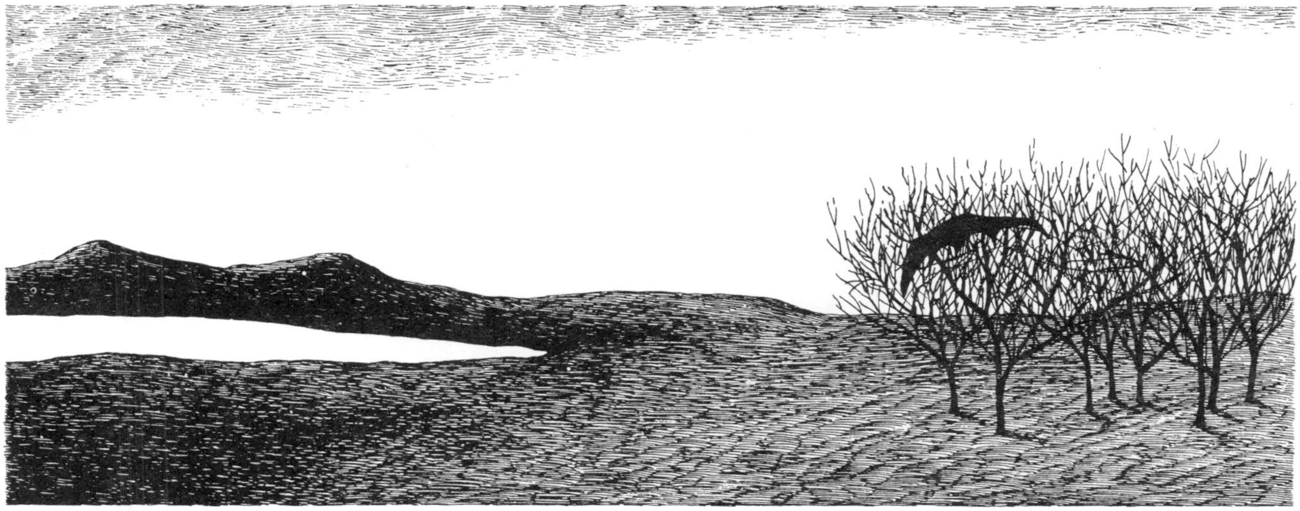

On the shore a bat, or possibly an umbrella,

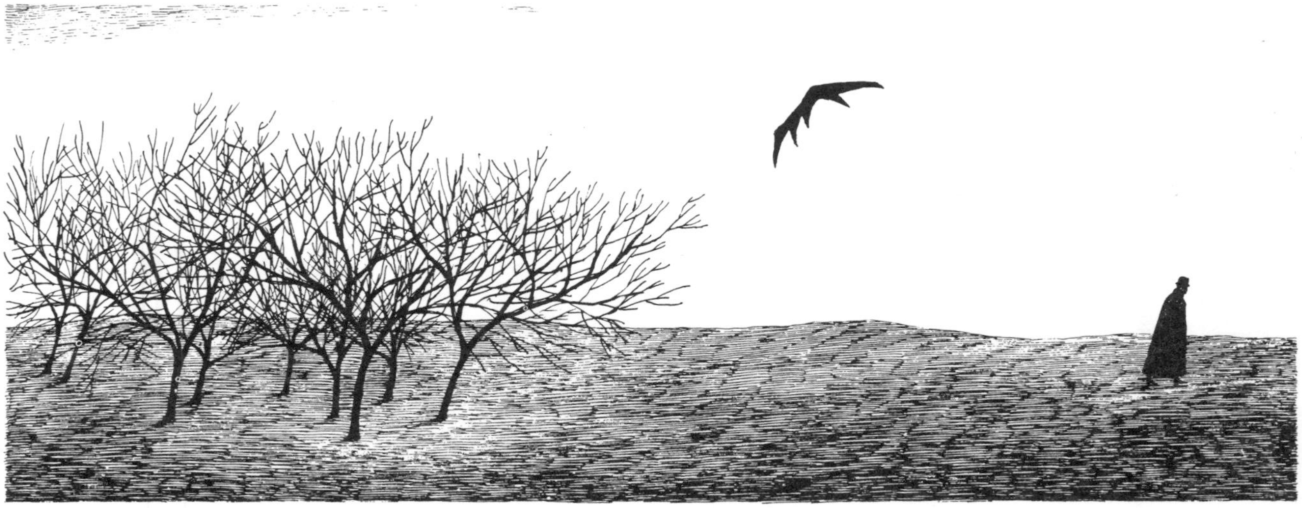

disengaged itself from the shrubbery,

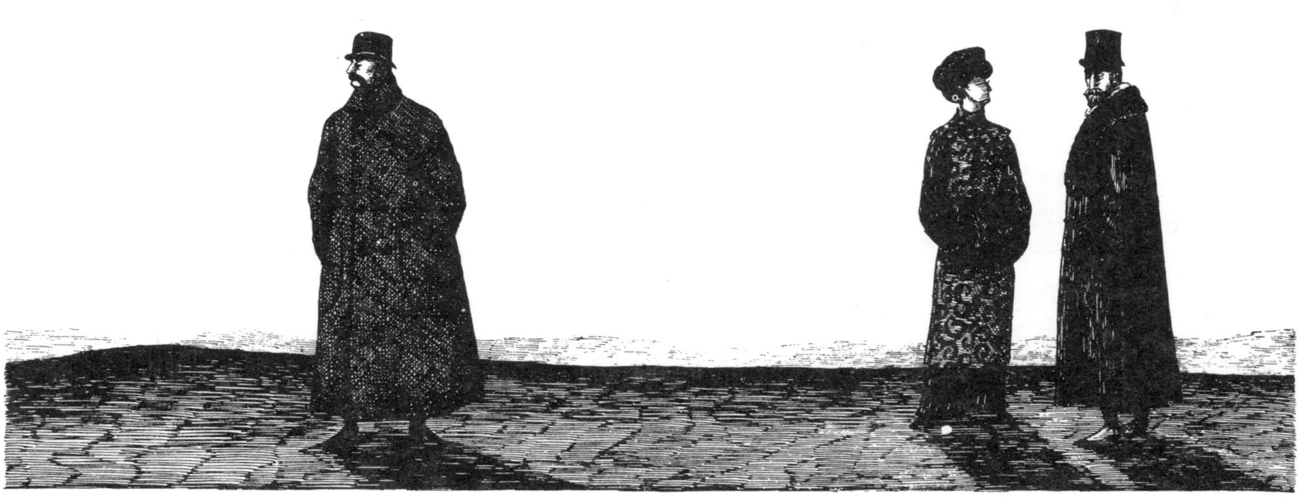

causing those nearby to recollect the miseries of childhood.

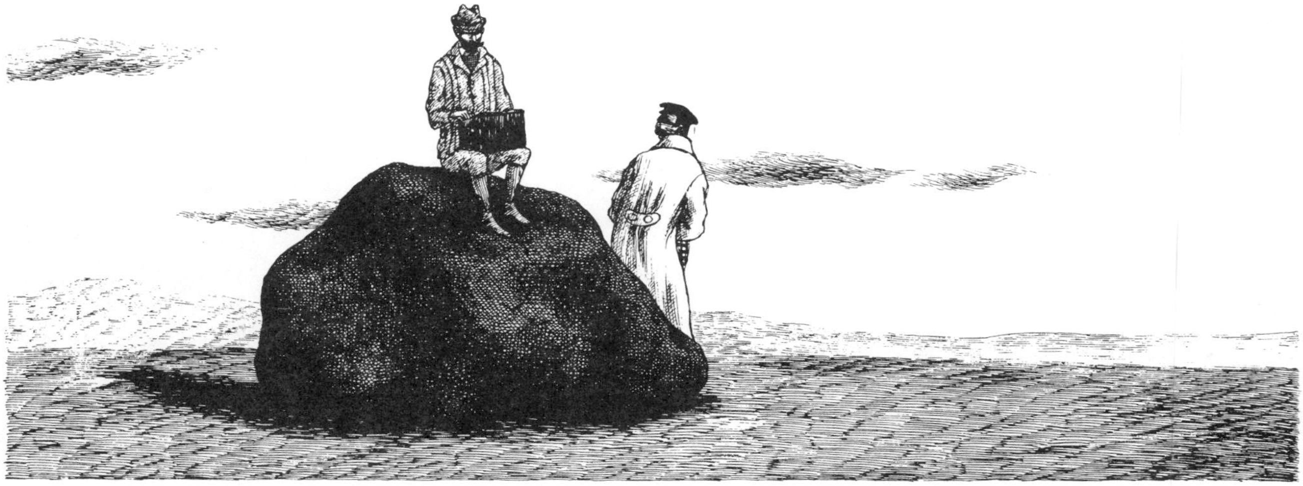

It now became apparent (despite the lack of library paste)

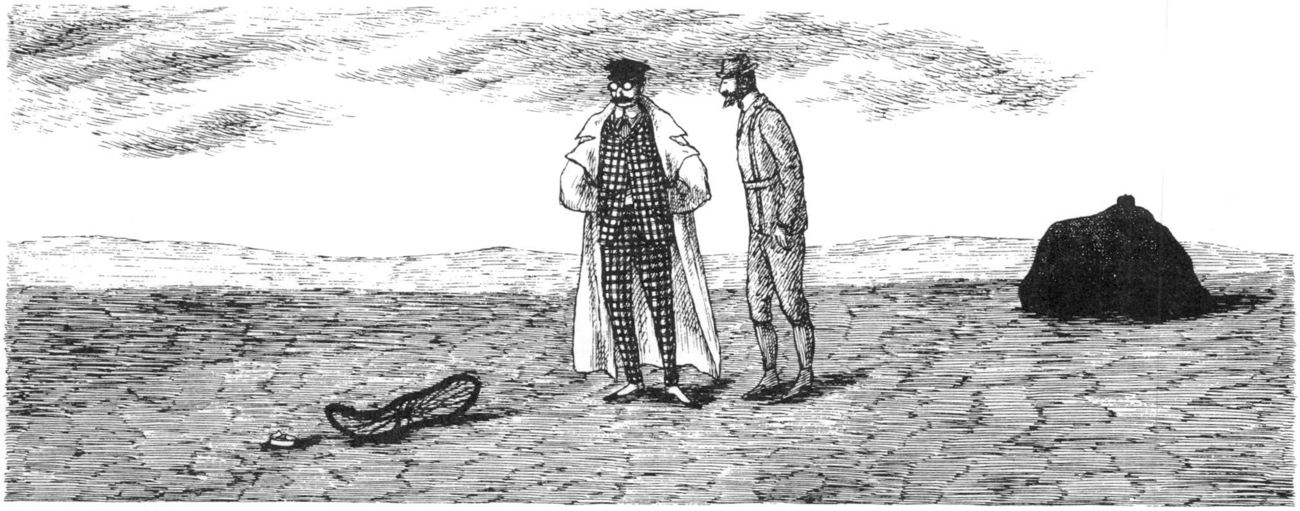

that something had happened to the vicar;

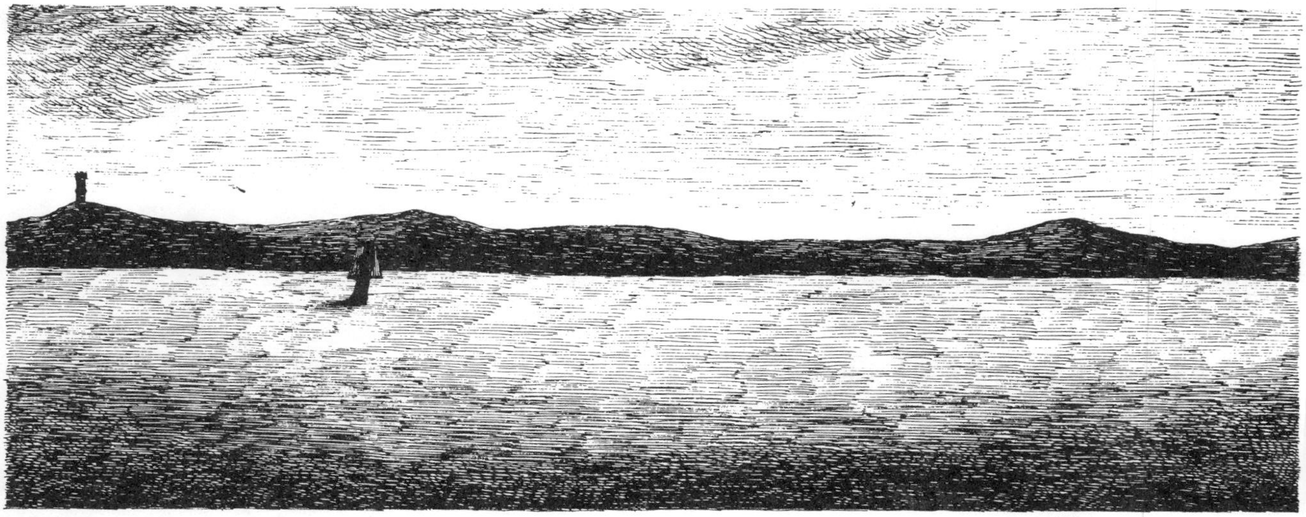

guns began to go off in the distance.

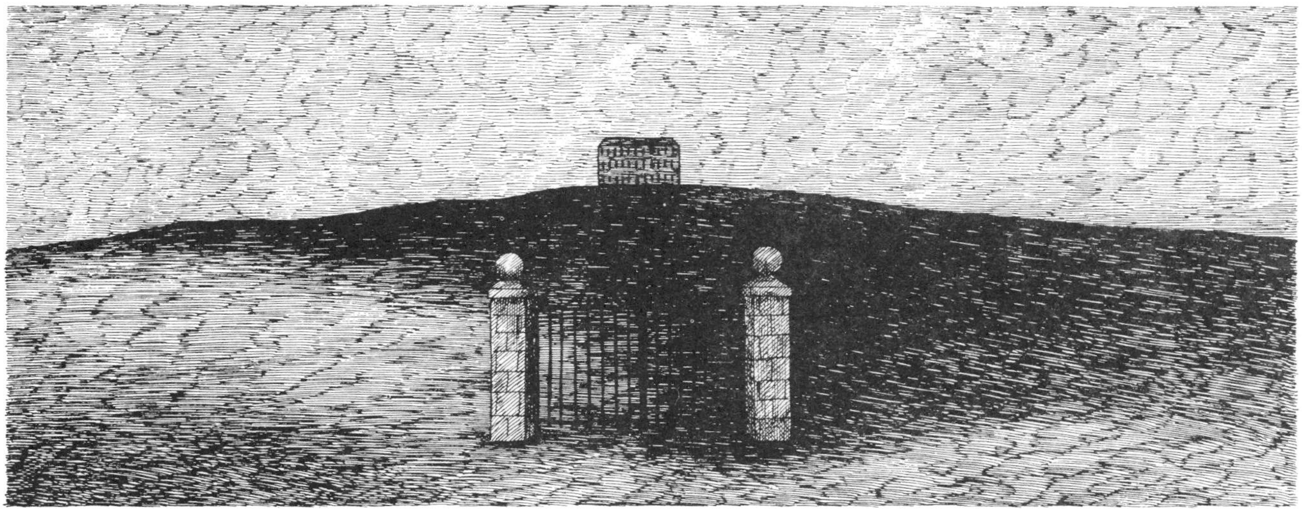

At twilight, however, no message had come from the asylum,

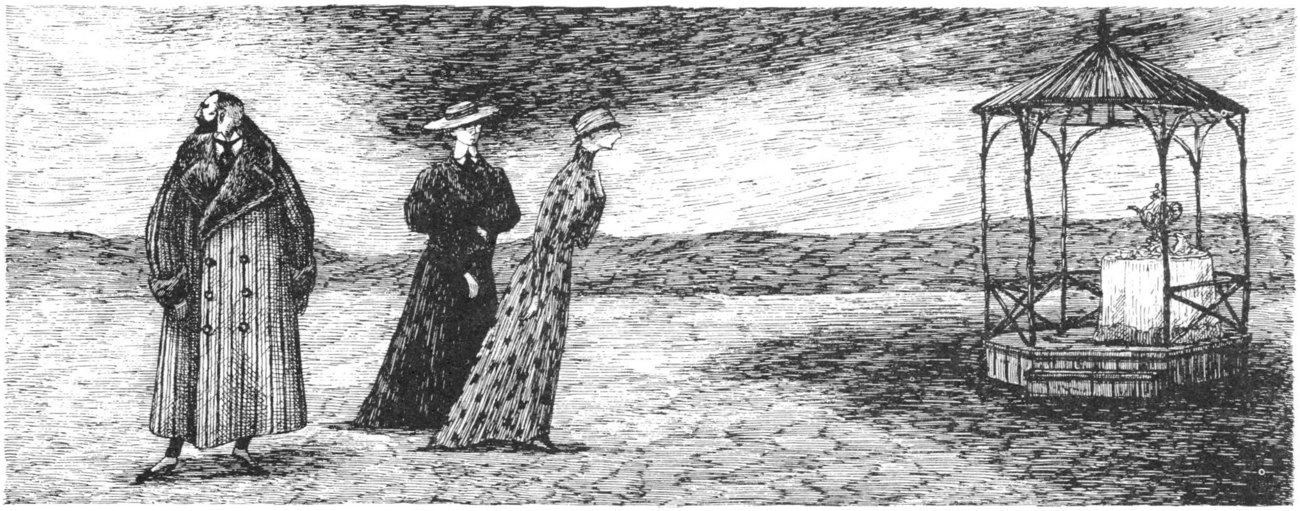

so the others retired to the kiosk,

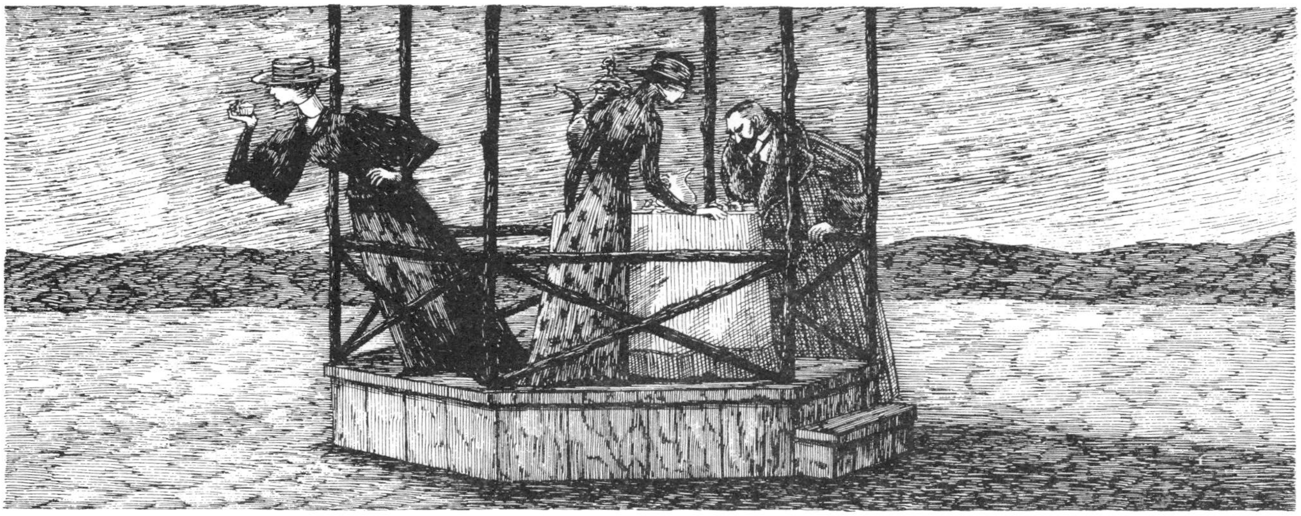

only to discover the cakes iced a peculiar shade of green

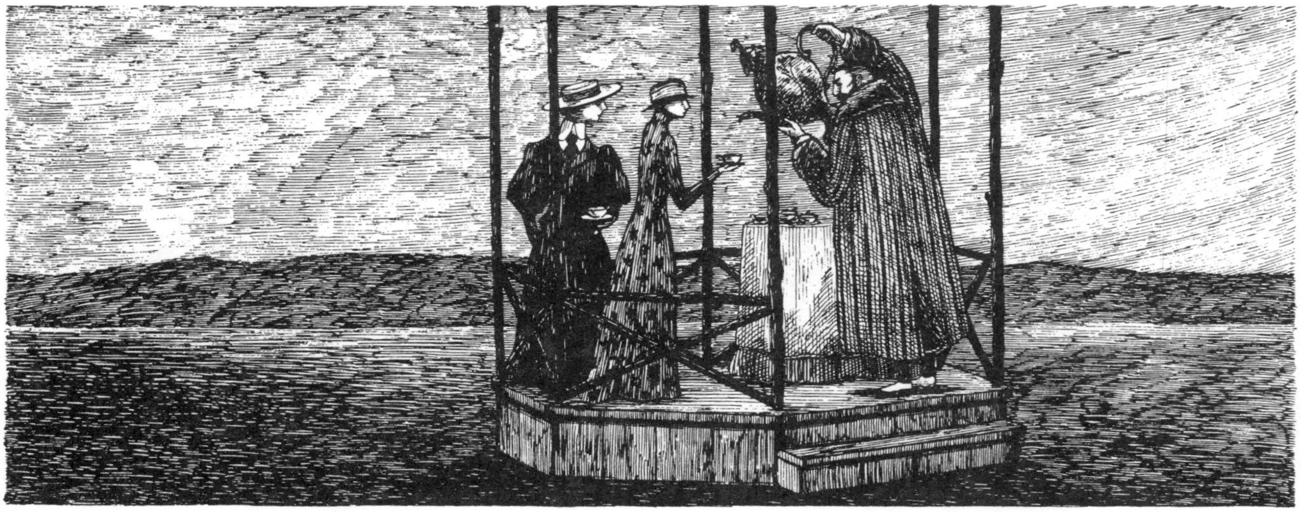

and the tea-urn empty

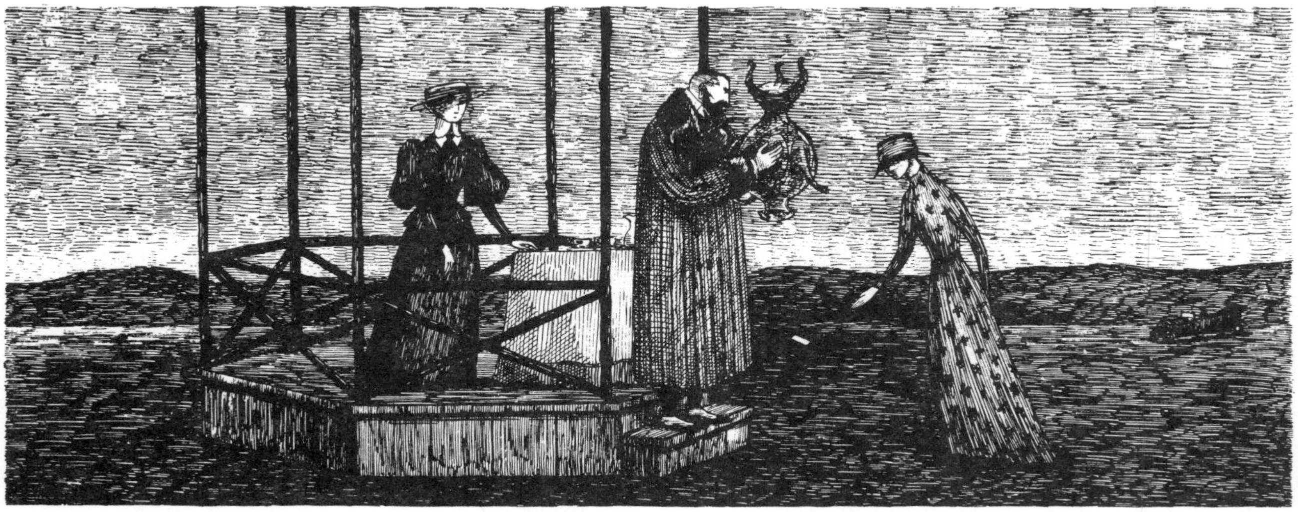

save for a card on which was written the single word:

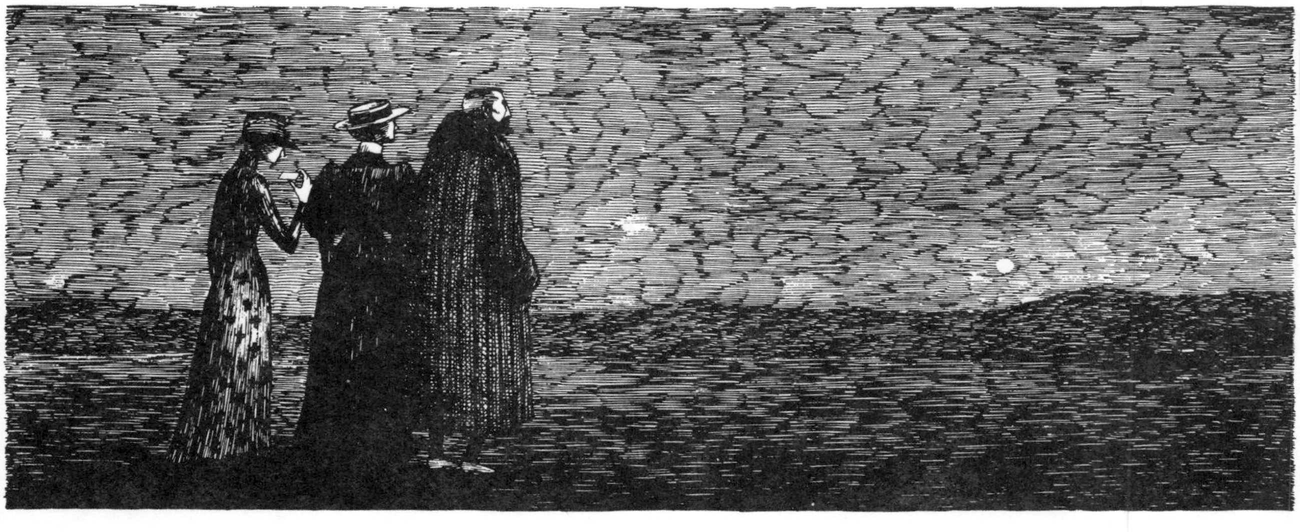

Farewell.

The BUG BOOK

by

EDWARD GOREY

There were once two blue bugs.

They lived in a teacup which had a piece missing from the rim.

They were frivolous, and often danced on the roof.

There were also three red bugs, who were cousins of the blue bugs.

They lived nearby, inside a blue bottle, which made them an interesting violet colour when they were at home.

They were house-proud, and frequently polished the glass on both sides.

There were also two yellow bugs, who were cousins of both the blue and red bugs.

They lived a little further off, on the topmost leaf but one of a plant.

They were pensive, and sometimes sat on the topmost leaf and looked into the distance.

All the bugs were on the friendliest possible terms and constantly went to call on each other

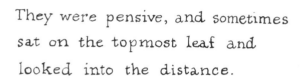

And went on excursions together

And had delightful parties.

And then one day a black bug, who was related to nobody, appeared in the neighbourhood.

The other bugs were dubious, but nevertheless made an attempt to be friendly.

It was not a success.

After that, the black bug broke up their parties

And waylaid them whenever they went visiting.

Social life came to a standstill.

A desperate secret meeting was held.

At last they decided on a plan.

The next morning they rushed
from their homes and dashed
to the top of a certain cliff.

The black bug followed them
to the foot of the cliff, where
he jumped up and down, and
shouted personal remarks.

Meanwhile, they were pushing
a large stone towards the edge.

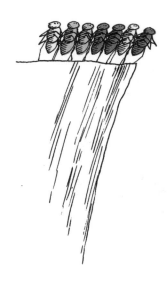

It went over, and almost
at once a horrid noise came
from below.

Presently they descended and
rolled aside the stone.

The black bug had been
squashed quite flat.

To whom it may concern

They slipped the remains
into an envelope

And left it propped against
the fatal stone to be mailed.

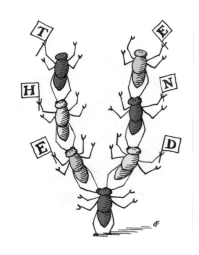

After which they had a party
complete with cake crumbs
and raspberry punch

And everyone enjoyed
himself immensely.

THE FATAL LOZENGE

An Apparition of her lover
She recognizes with dismay;
And later on she will discover
That he himself had died today.

The Baby, lying meek and quiet
Upon the customary rug,
Has dreams about rampage and riot,
And will grow up to be a thug.

The Cad decides he has grown weary
Of this affair, and that is that;
And so he tells her just how dreary
He thinks she is, then leaves the flat.

The Drudge expends her life in mopping,
In emptying and filling pails;
And she will do so, never stopping,
Until her strength entirely fails.

The Effigy, got up with clothing
    Abstracted from the victim's room,
Is raised aloft to cheers of loathing
    Before it meets a flaming doom.

The Fetishist gets out the hassock,
    Turns down the lamp, and bolts the door;
Then in galoshes and a cassock,
    He worships It upon the floor.

The Governess up in the attic
    Attempts to make a cup of tea;
Her mind grows daily more erratic
    From cold and hunger and ennui.

The Hermit lives among the boulders,
    He wears no garment but a sack;
By slow degrees his reason moulders,
    The sun has long since burnt him black.

The Invalid *wakes up in terror*
   To feel his toes becoming numb;
The doctor's made another error —
   What unknown symptoms are to come?

The Journalist *surveys the slaughter,*
   The best in years without a doubt;
He pours himself a gin-and-water
   And wonders how it came about.

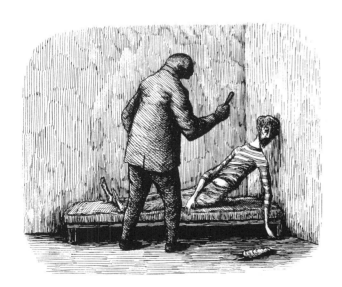

The Keeper, *when it's time for luncheon,*
   Flings down his charge upon the bed,
And taking out a home-made truncheon,
   Belabours him about the head.

The Lazar, *blessed with an appearance*
   Enough to give the strongest qualms,
Has little need of perseverance
   In prompting a display of alms.

The Magnate *waits upon the pavement*
  For his enormous limousine,
And ponders further child-enslavement
  And other projects still more mean.

The Nun *is fearfully bedevilled:*
  She runs about and moans and shrieks;
Her flesh is bruised, her clothes dishevelled:
  She's been like this for weeks and weeks.

The Orphan *whom there's none to cherish*
  Strays through the gloom on naked feet;
She presently will fall, and perish
  Unnoticed in some squalid street.

The Proctor *buys a pupil ices,*
  And hopes the boy will not resist
When he attempts to practise vices
  Few people even know exist.

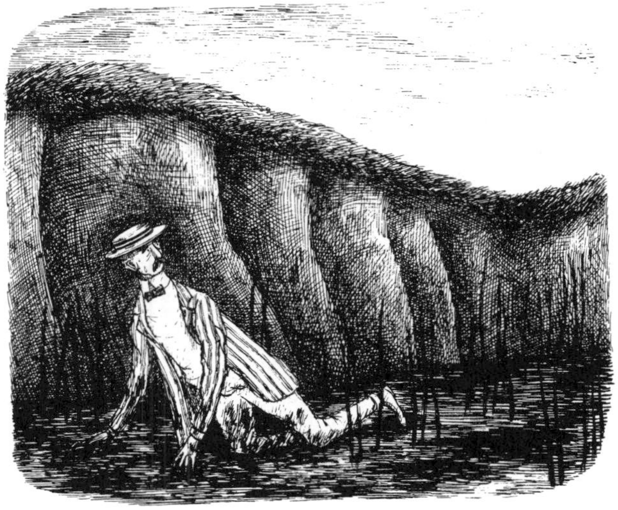

The Quarry, *fleeing from the outing,*
Sinks panting in the reeds and mud;
And hearkens to the distant shouting
That tells him they are out for blood.

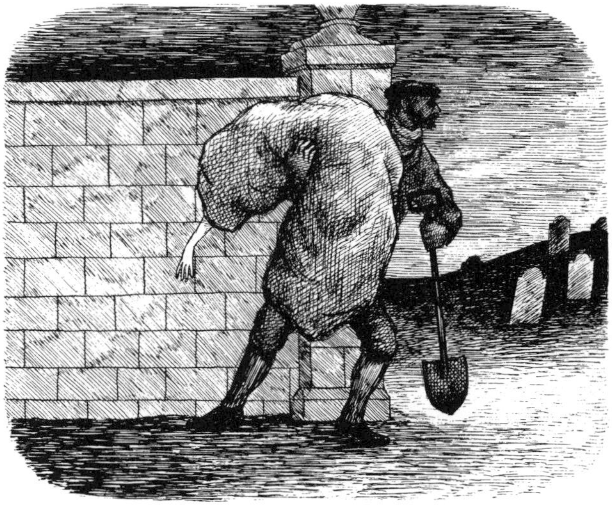

The Resurrectionist *goes plying*
Without ado his simple trade;
Material is always dying
And got with nothing but a spade.

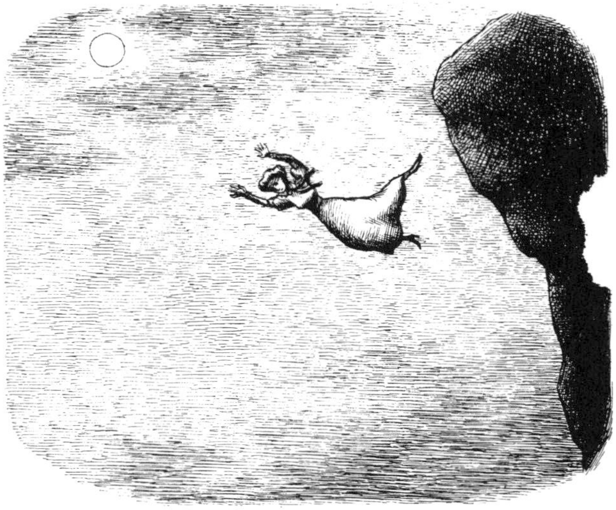

The Suicide, *as she is falling,*
Illuminated by the moon,
Regrets her act, and finds appalling
The thought she will be dead so soon.

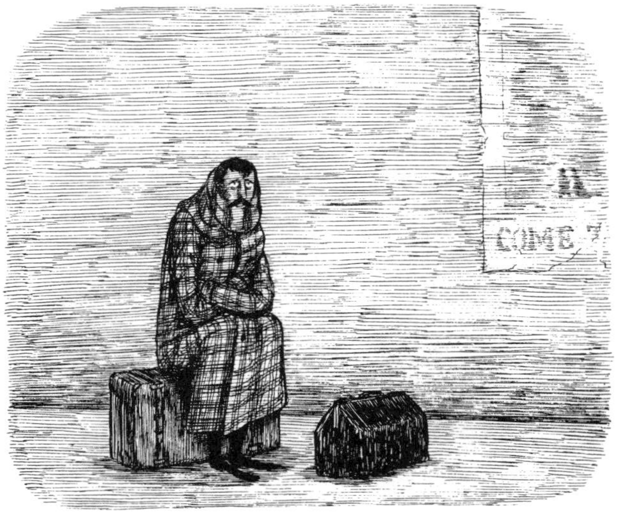
COME

The Tourist *huddles in the station*
While slowly night gives way to dawn;
He finds a certain fascination
In knowing all the trains are gone.

The sight of Uncle gives no pleasure,
  But rather causes much alarm:
The children know that at his leisure
  He plans to have them come to harm.

The Visitor was somewhat pensive
  When she arrived to pay a call;
But now she's faint and apprehensive
  From hours of waiting in the hall.

The Wanton, though she knows its dangers,
  Must needs smear kohl about her eyes,
And wake the interest of strangers
  With long-drawn, hoarse, erotic sighs.

The Xenophobe grabs at the table,
  He feels his toes and fingers curl;
For he is only barely able
  To keep from striking down the girl.

The Yegg on rubber soles comes creeping
   Inside the house when it is late,
And while the occupants are sleeping,
   Removes the heirlooms and the plate.

The Zouave used to war and battle
   Would sooner take a life than not:
It scarcely has begun to prattle
   When he impales the hapless tot.

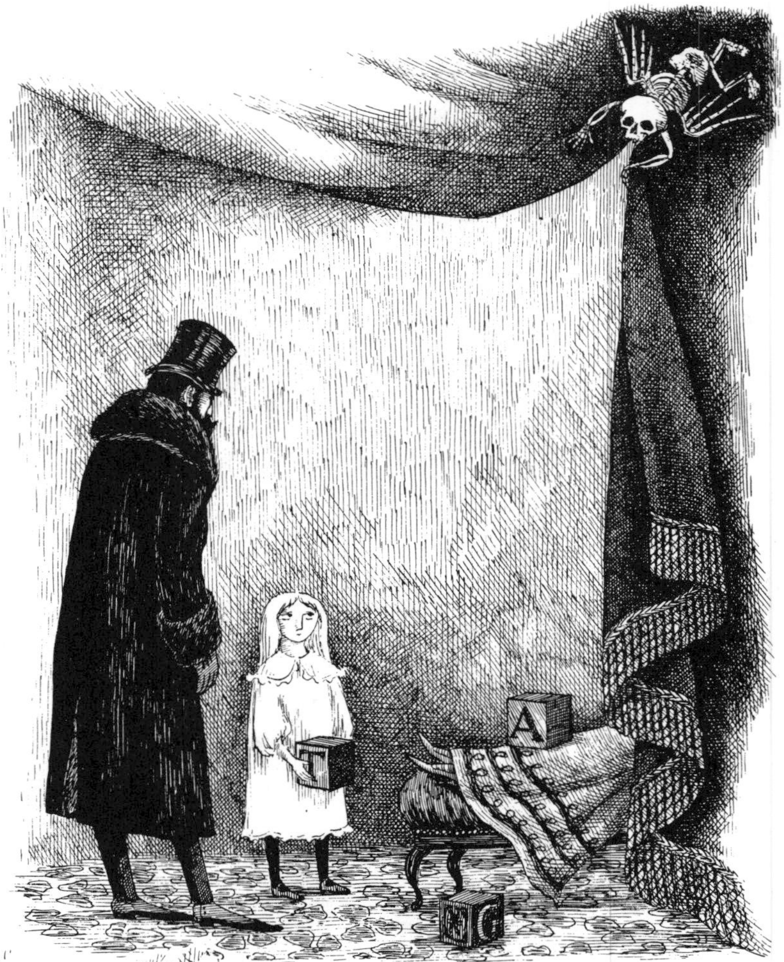

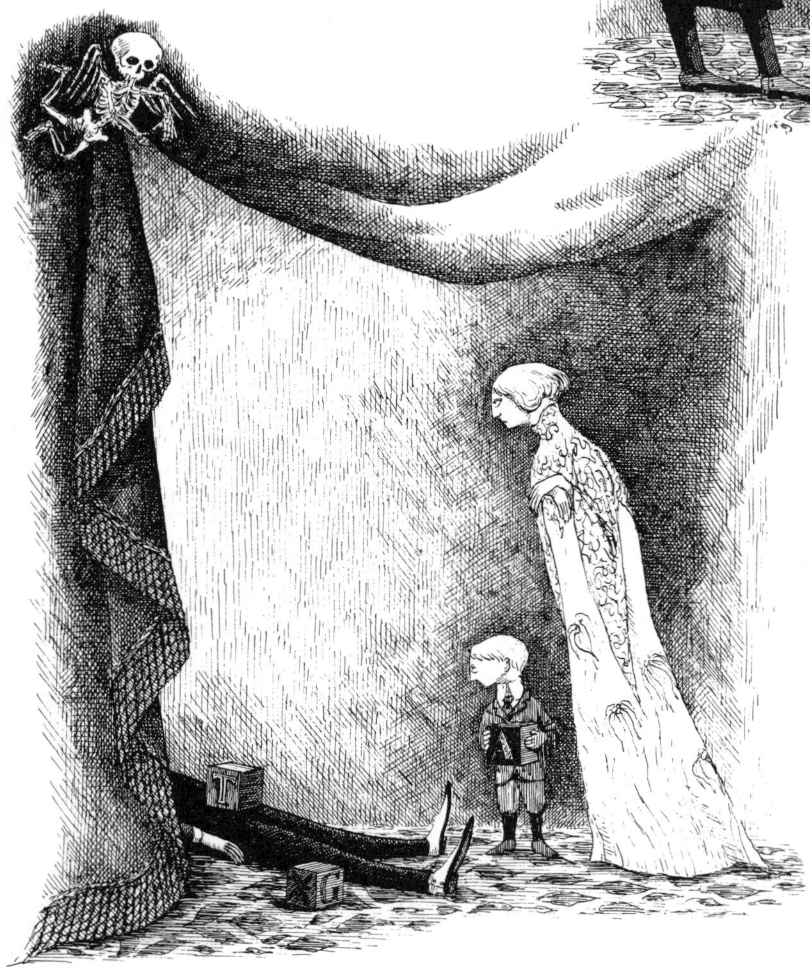

THE HAPLESS CHILD

There was once a little girl named Charlotte Sophia.

Her parents were kind and well-to-do.

She had a doll whom she called Hortense.

One day her father, a colonel in the army, was
ordered to Africa.

Several months later he was reported killed in a native uprising.

Her mother fell into a decline that proved fatal.

Her only other relative, an uncle, was brained by a piece of masonry.

Charlotte Sophia was left in the hands of the family lawyer.

He at once put her into a boarding-school.

There she was punished by the teachers for things she hadn't done.

Hortense was torn limb from limb by the other pupils.

During the day Charlotte Sophia hid as much as possible.

At night she lay awake weeping and weeping.

When she could bear it no longer she fled from the school at dawn.

She soon lost consciousness and sank to the pavement.

A man came and took the locket with her parents' pictures inside.

Another man came from the opposite direction and carried her off.

He brought her to a low place.

He sold her to a drunken brute.

Charlotte Sophia was put to work making artificial flowers.

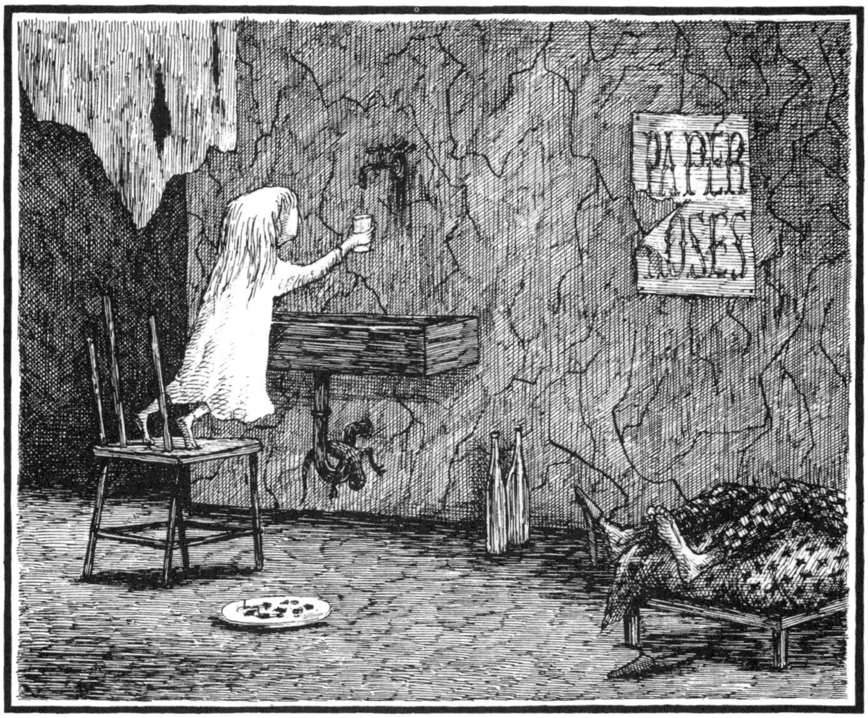
PAPER
OSES

She lived on scraps and tap-water.

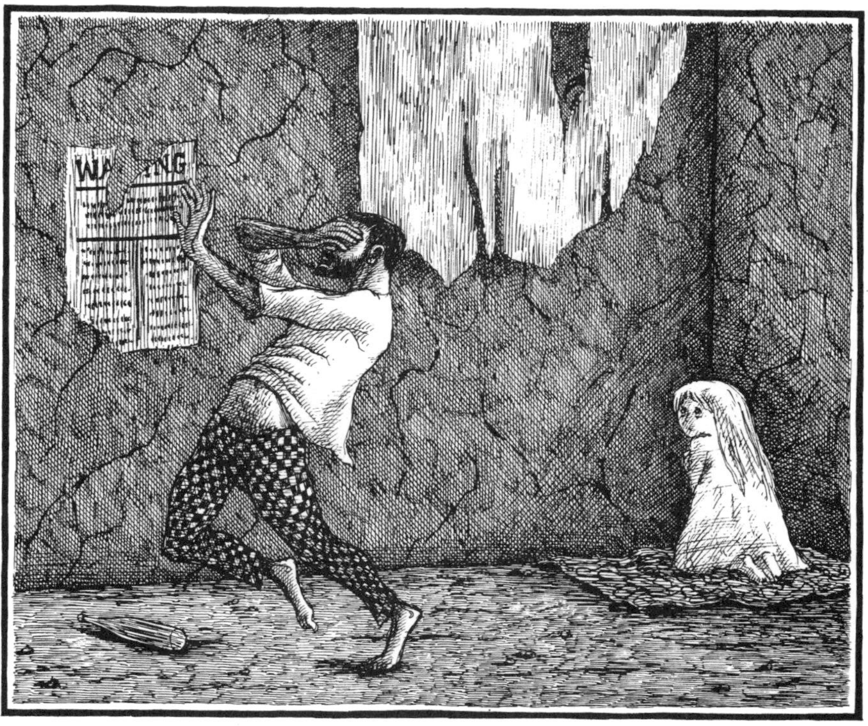
WA NG

From time to time the brute got the horrors.

Charlotte Sophia's eyesight began to fail rapidly.

*Meanwhile, her father, who was not dead after all,
returned home.*

*Every day he motored through the streets searching
for her.*

At last the brute went off his head.

Charlotte Sophia, now almost blind, ran into the street.

She was at once struck down by a car.

Her father got out to look at the dying child.

She was so changed, he did not recognize her.

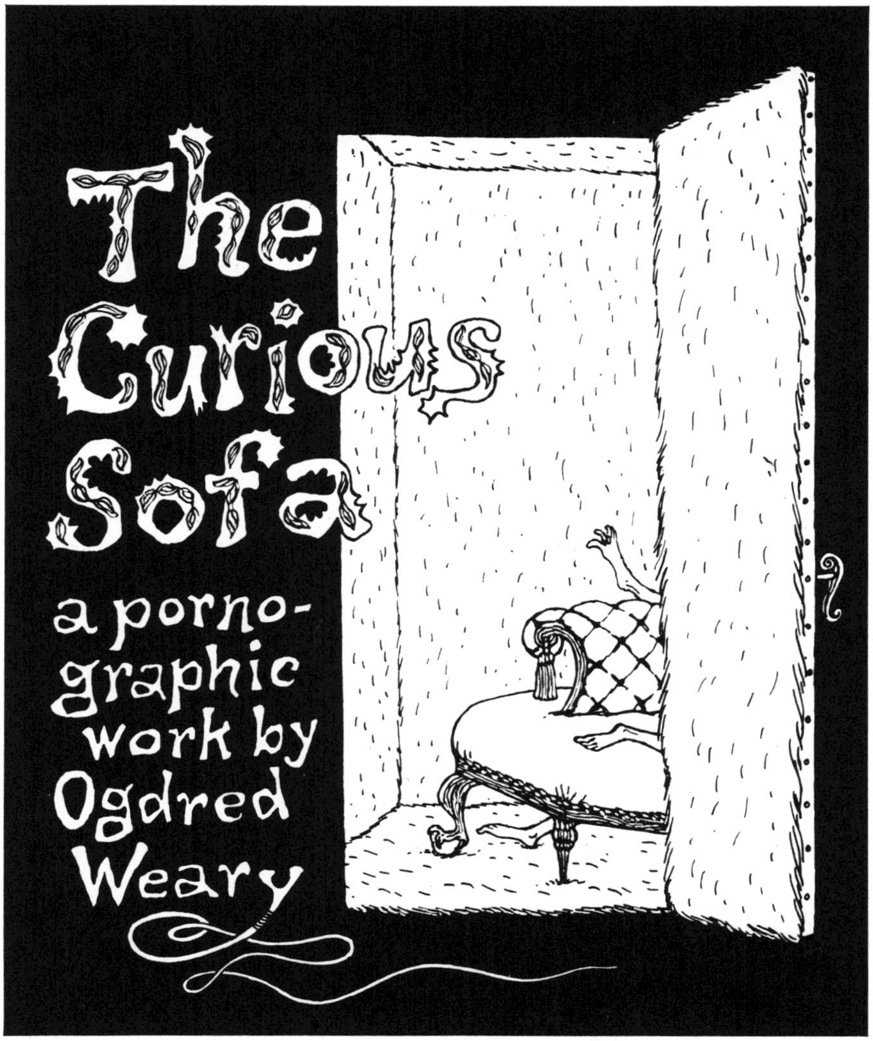
The Curious Sofa
a porno-
graphic
work by
Ogdred
Weary

Alice was eating grapes in the park when Herbert, an extremely well-endowed young man, introduced himself to her.

He invited her to go for a ride in a taxi-cab, on the floor of which they did something Alice had never done before.

After they had done it several times in different ways, Herbert suggested that Alice tidy up at the home of his aunt, Lady Celia, who welcomed them with great cordiality.

Lady Celia led Alice to her boudoir, where she requested the girl to perform a rather surprising service.

Downstairs the three of them played a most amusing game of Herbert's own invention called "Thumbfumble." They then sat down to a sumptuous tea.

After he had finished the washing-up, Albert, the butler, an unusually well-formed man of middle age, joined them for another frolic. Herbert and Lady Celia had little difficulty in persuading Alice to spend a few days with them.

In the interval before dinner she perused an album of instructive chromolithographs entitled ‚Die Sieben und Dreißig Wollüste‘ which Lady Celia had thoughtfully set out.

Colonel Gilbert and his wife, Louise, came in after dinner; both of them had wooden legs, with which they could do all sorts of entertaining tricks.

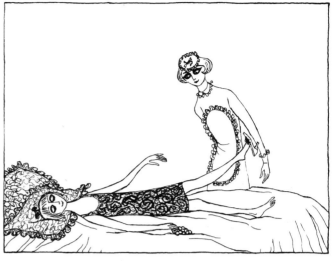

The evening was a huge success, in spite of someone fainting from time to time.

Alice, quite exhausted, was helped to bed by Lady Celia's French maid, Lise, whom she found delightfully sympathetic.

The next morning she was wakened in a novel fashion by Lady Celia in time for elevenses.

Looking out the window she saw Herbert, Albert, and Harold, the gardener, an exceptionally well-made youth, disporting themselves on the lawn.

They were soon joined by Donald, Herbert's singularly well-favoured sheepdog, and many were the giggles and barks that came from the shrubbery.

They called up to Alice, who, having put on an ingeniously constructed bathing slip, met them in the pool.

At luncheon, which was alfresco, Lady Celia announced they were invited to the Gilberts for the weekend.

To beguile the tedium of the journey, Albert read aloud from Volume Eleven of the "Encyclopedia of Unimaginable Customs."

As they drove up to the house, Lucy, the Gilbert's daughter, and Gerald, her fiancé, an uncommonly well-shaped older man, emerged from an ornamental urn.

That evening in the library Scylla, one of the guests who had certain anatomical peculiarities, demonstrated the "Lithuanian Typewriter," assisted by Ronald and Robert, two remarkably well-set-up young men from the village.

Later Reginald, another remarkably well-set-up young man from the village, provided everyone with the most astonishing little device.

Still later Gerald did a terrible thing to Elsie with a saucepan.

The party split into twos and threes before retiring.

At breakfast it was learned that Elsie had expired during the night, and gloom descended on everybody.

When a change of scene was proposed, Lady Celia suggested a visit to the nearby seat of Sir Egbert, a dear friend of her youth.

When they got there, they found Sir Egbert, an extraordinarily well-proportioned old gentleman, and his friend, Louie, having a romp on the terrace.

They all went indoors and worked up some most intriguing charades.

During the light buffet supper Louie did a dance with a boa.

Sir Egbert offered to show them his famous sofa. Alice felt a shudder of nameless apprehension.

It stood in a windowless room lined with polar bear fur and otherwise empty; it was upholstered in scarlet velvet, and had nine legs and seven arms.

As soon as everybody had crowded into the room, Sir Egbert fastened shut the door, and started up the machinery inside the sofa.

When Alice saw what was about to happen, she began to scream uncontrollably....

THE WILLOWDALE HANDCAR

BY EDWARD GOREY

OR

THE RETURN OF THE BLACK DOLL

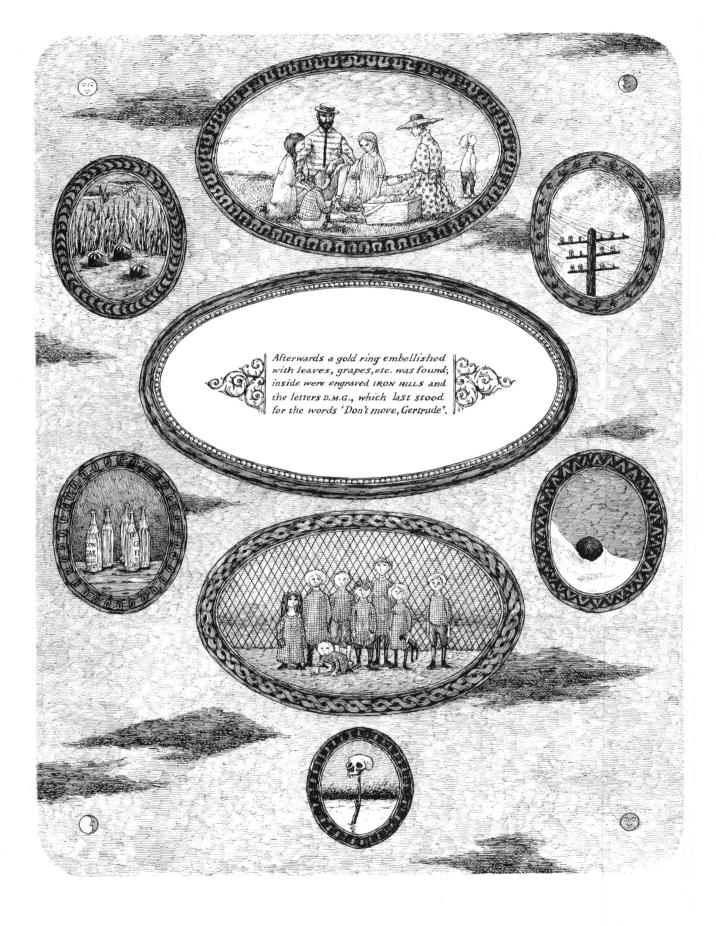

Afterwards a gold ring embellished
with leaves, grapes, etc. was found;
inside were engraved IRON HILLS and
the letters D.M.G., which last stood
for the words 'Don't move, Gertrude'.

One summer afternoon in Willowdale Edna,
Harry, and Sam wandered down to the railroad
station to see if anything was doing.

There was nothing on the platform but some empty
crates. 'Look!' said Harry, pointing to a handcar
on the siding. 'Let's take it and go for a ride.'

Soon they were flying along the tracks at a great rate. Little Grace Sprocket, playing in a home-made mud puddle, watched them go by with longing.

At Bogus Corners, the next town down the line, they stopped to buy soda pop and gingersnaps at Mr Queevil's store. 'How are things over in Willowdale?' he asked. 'Dull' they said.

A few minutes after they were on their way again,
they saw a house burning down in a field.
'Whooee!' said Sam. 'The engines will never
be in time to save it.'

The next morning they wrote postcards to everybody, telling them what they were doing and
didn't know exactly when they would be back.

At 10:17 the Turnip Valley Express rushed past.
A frantic face was pressed against a window
of the parlor car.

'Gracious!' said Edna. 'I believe that was Nellie
Flim. We were chums at Miss Underfoot's Seminary.
I wonder what can have been the matter.'

In Chutney Falls they hunted up the cemetery and peered at the tombstones of Harry's mother's family.

Later they ran into Nellie's beau, Dick Hammerclaw, the local telegraph operator. He asked if they'd seen her. He seemed upset.

Near Gristleburg they saw a palatial mansion on a bluff. 'That's O Altitudo,' said Sam, 'the home of Titus W. Blotter, the financier. I saw a picture in a magazine.'

Several days later a touring car drew up alongside them. The driver called out something unintelligible concerning Dick before he shot away out of sight.

*An undated fragment of the 'Willowdale Triangle'
they found caught in a tie informed them that
Wobbling Rock had finally fallen on a family
having a picnic.*

*In Dogear Junction they paid a call on Edna's
cousins, the Zeph Claggs. He showed them a few
of the prizes from his collection of over 7,000 glass
telephone-pole insulators.*

The following week Mount Smith came into
view in the distance; dark clouds were piling
up behind it.

During the thunderstorm that ensued, a flash
of lightning revealed a figure creeping up
the embankment.

Some months went by, and still they had not returned to Willowdale.

They visited the ruins of the Crampton vinegar works, which had been destroyed by a mysterious explosion the preceding fall.

At Wunksieville they rescued an infant who was
hanging from a hook intended for mailbags.

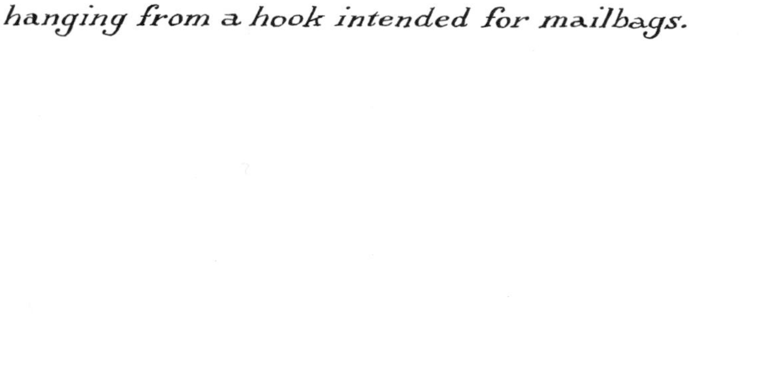

'How much she resembles Nellie!' said Edna. They
turned her over to the matron of the orphanage
in Stovepipe City.

From the trestle over Peevish Gorge they spied the wreck of a touring car at the bottom. 'I don't see Dick's friend anywhere,' said Harry.

In Violet Springs they learned that Mrs Regera Dowdy was not receiving visitors, but through a window they were able to see the desk on which she wrote her poems.

As they were going along the edge of the Sogmush River, they passed a man in a canoe. 'If I'm not mistaken,' said Edna, 'he was lurking inside the vinegar works'.

Between West Elbow and Penetralia they almost ran over someone who was tied to the track. It proved to be Nellie.

Despite their entreaties, she insisted on being
left at the first grade crossing, where she got
on a bicycle and rode away.

That evening they attended a baked-bean supper
at the Halfbath Methodist Church. 'They're
all right,' said Sam, 'but they're not a patch
on Mrs Umlaut's back home'.

A week later they noticed someone who might be Nellie walking in the grounds of the Weedhaven Laughing Academy.

On Sunday afternoon they saw Titus W. Blotter in his shirtsleeves plunge into the Great Trackless Swamp.

In Hiccupboro they counted the cannon balls in the pyramids on the courthouse lawn.

At sunset they entered a tunnel in the Iron Hills and did not come out the other end.

THE
VINEGAR
WORKS

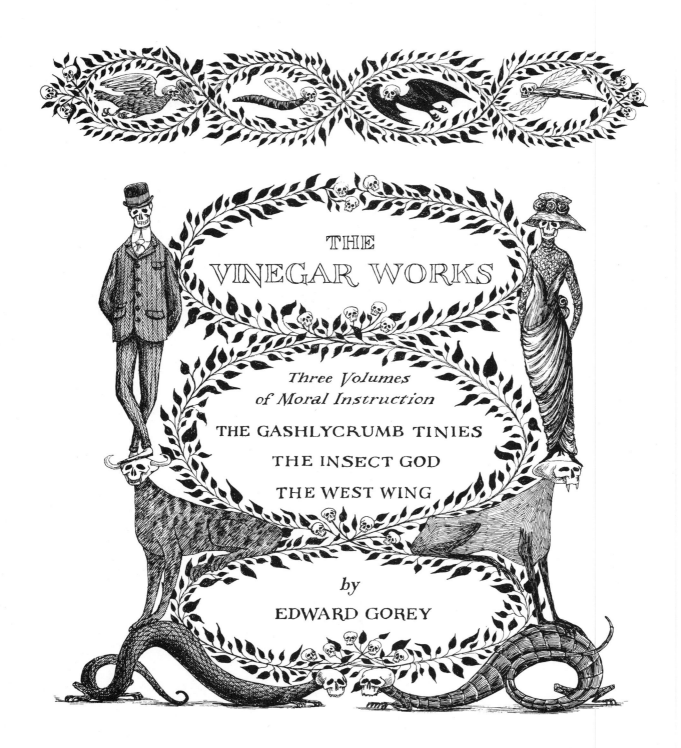

THE VINEGAR WORKS

Three Volumes
of Moral Instruction

THE GASHLYCRUMB TINIES

THE INSECT GOD

THE WEST WING

by

EDWARD GOREY

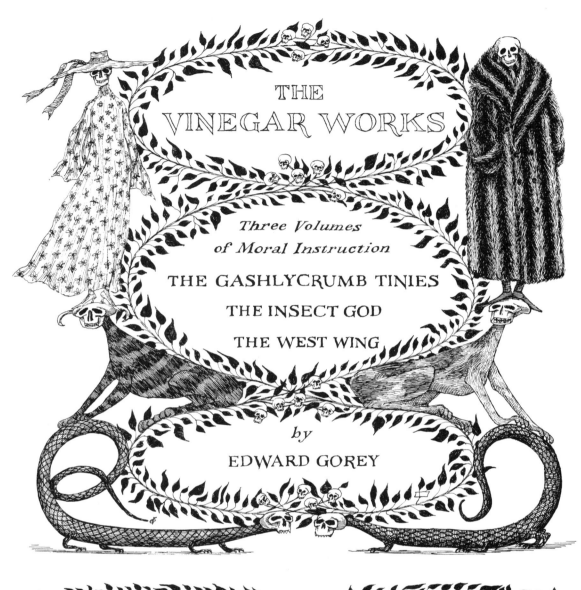

THE VINEGAR WORKS

*Three Volumes
of Moral Instruction*

THE GASHLYCRUMB TINIES
THE INSECT GOD
THE WEST WING

by

EDWARD GOREY

THE GASHLYCRUMB TINIES

A is for AMY who fell down the stairs

B is for BASIL assaulted by bears

C is for CLARA who wasted away

D is for DESMOND thrown out of a sleigh

E is for ERNEST who choked on a peach

F is for FANNY sucked dry by a leech

G is for GEORGE smothered under a rug

H is for HECTOR done in by a thug

I is for IDA who drowned in a lake

J is for JAMES who took lye by mistake

K is for KATE who was struck with an axe

L is for LEO who swallowed some tacks

M is for MAUD who was swept out to sea

N is for NEVILLE who died of ennui

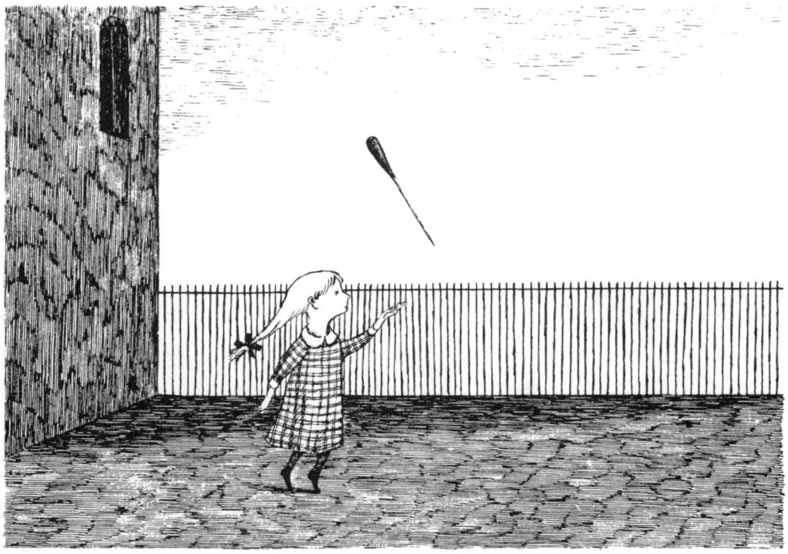

O is for OLIVE run through with an awl

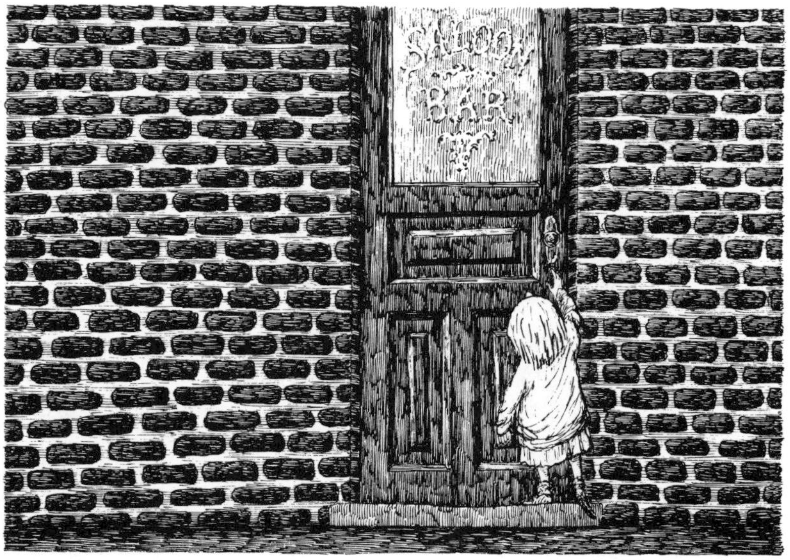
BAR

P is for PRUE trampled flat in a brawl

Q is for QUENTIN who sank in a mire

R is for RHODA consumed by a fire

S is for SUSAN who perished of fits

T is for TITUS who flew into bits

U is for UNA who slipped down a drain

V is for VICTOR squashed under a train

W is for WINNIE embedded in ice

X is for XERXES devoured by mice

Y is for YORICK whose head was knocked in

Z is for ZILLAH who drank too much gin

THE INSECT GOD

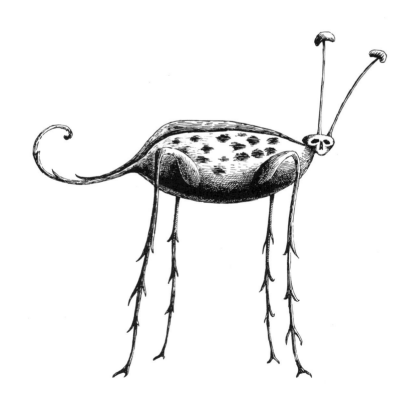

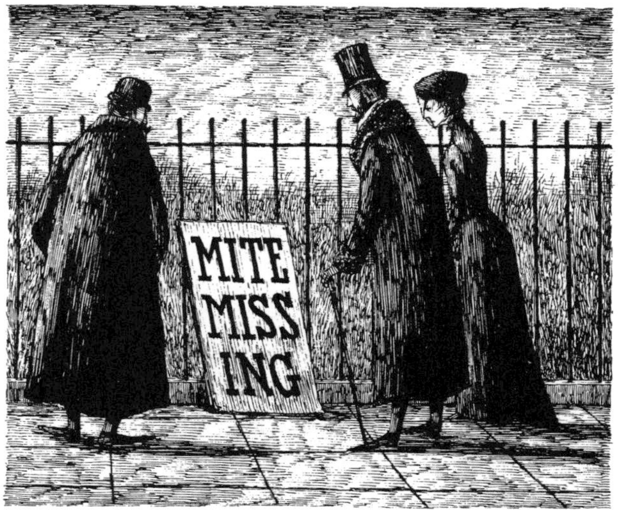
MITE
MISS
ING

O what has become of Millicent Frastley?
Is there any hope that she's still alive?
Why haven't they found her? It's rather ghastly
To think that the child was not yet five.

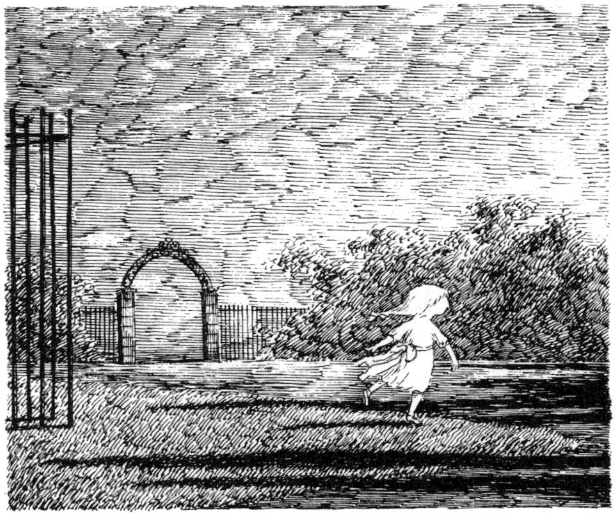

The dear little thing was last seen playing
Alone by herself at the edge of the park;
There was no one with her to keep her from straying
Away in the shadows and oncoming dark.

Before she could do so, a silent and glittering
    Black motor drew up where she sat nibbling grass;
From within came a nearly inaudible twittering,
    A tiny green face peered out through the glass.

She was ready to flee, when the figure beckoned;
    An arm with two elbows held out a tin
Full of cinnamon balls; she paused; a second
    Reached out as she took one, and lifted her in.

The nurse was discovered collapsed in some shrubbery,
  But her reappearance was not much use;
Her eyes were askew, her extremities rubbery,
  Her clothing was stained with a brownish juice.

She was questioned in hopes of her answers revealing
  What had happened; she merely repeatedly said
'I hear them walking about on the ceiling'.
  She had gone irretrievably out of her head.

O feelings of horror, resentment, and pity
  For things, which so seldom turn out for the best:
The car, unobserved, sped away from the city
  As the last of the light died out in the west.

The Frastleys grew sick with apprehension,
  Which a heavy tea only served to increase;
Though they felt it was scarcely genteel to mention
  The loss of their child, they called in the police.

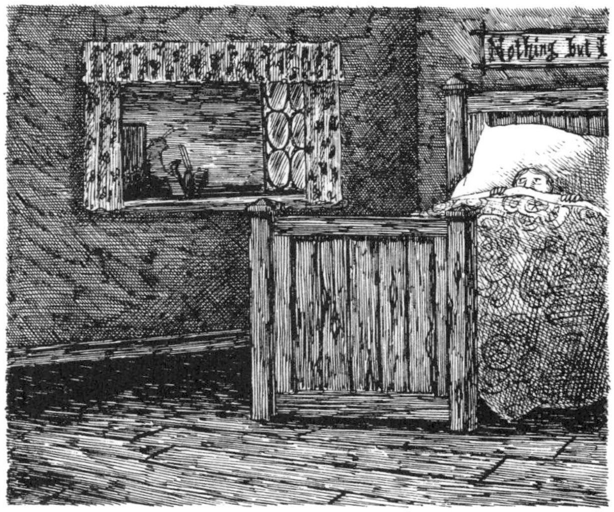
Nothing but

Through unvisited hamlets the car went creeping,
With its head lamps unlit and its curtains drawn;
Those natives who happened not to be sleeping
Heard it pass, and lay awake until dawn.

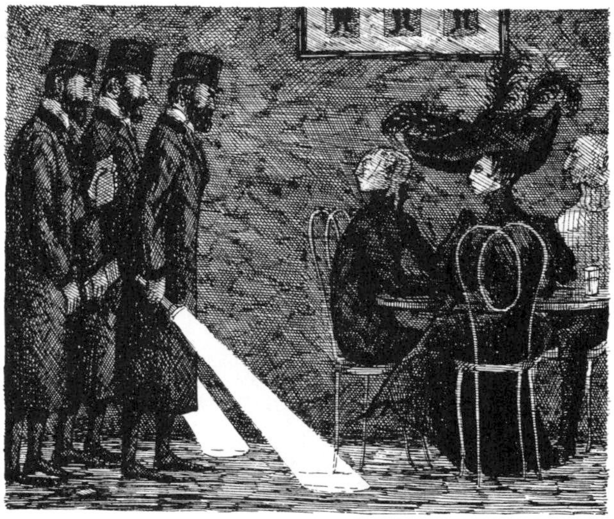

The police with their torches and notebooks descended
On the haunts of the underworld, looking for clues;
In spite of their praiseworthy efforts, they ended
With nothing at all in the way of news.

The car, after hours and hours of travel,
  Arrived at a gate in an endless wall;
It rolled up a drive and stopped on the gravel
  At the foot of a vast and crumbling hall.

As the night wore away hope started to languish
  And soon was replaced by all manner of fears;
The family twisted their fingers in anguish,
  Or got them all damp from the flow of their tears.

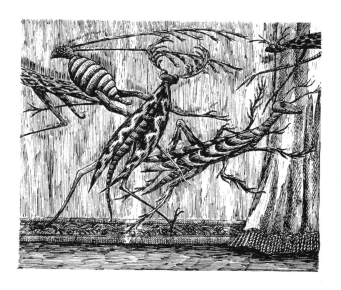

They removed the child to the ball-room, whose hangings
    And mirrors were streaked with a luminous slime;
They leapt through the air with buzzings and twangings
    To work themselves up to a ritual crime.

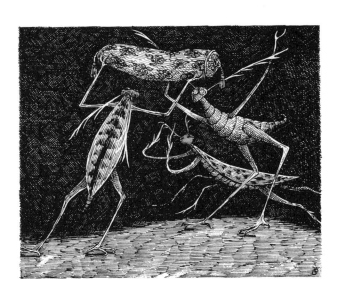

They stunned her, and stripped off her garments, and lastly
    They stuffed her inside a kind of pod;
And then it was that Millicent Frastley
    Was sacrificed to THE INSECT GOD.

THE WEST WING *by* EDWARD GOREY

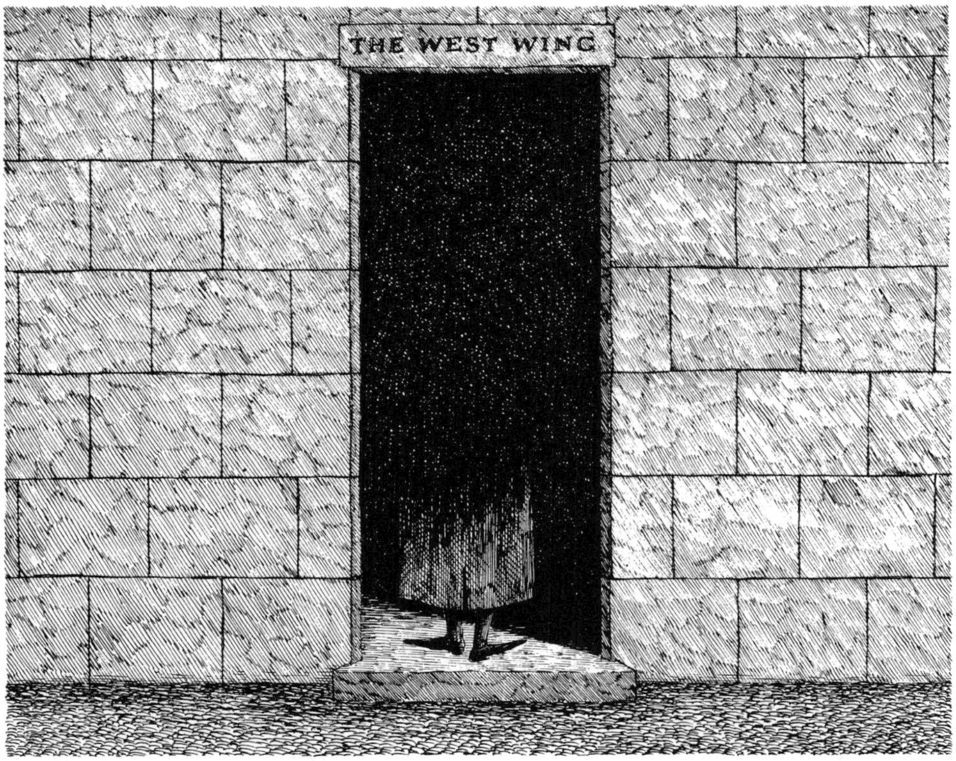
THE WEST WING

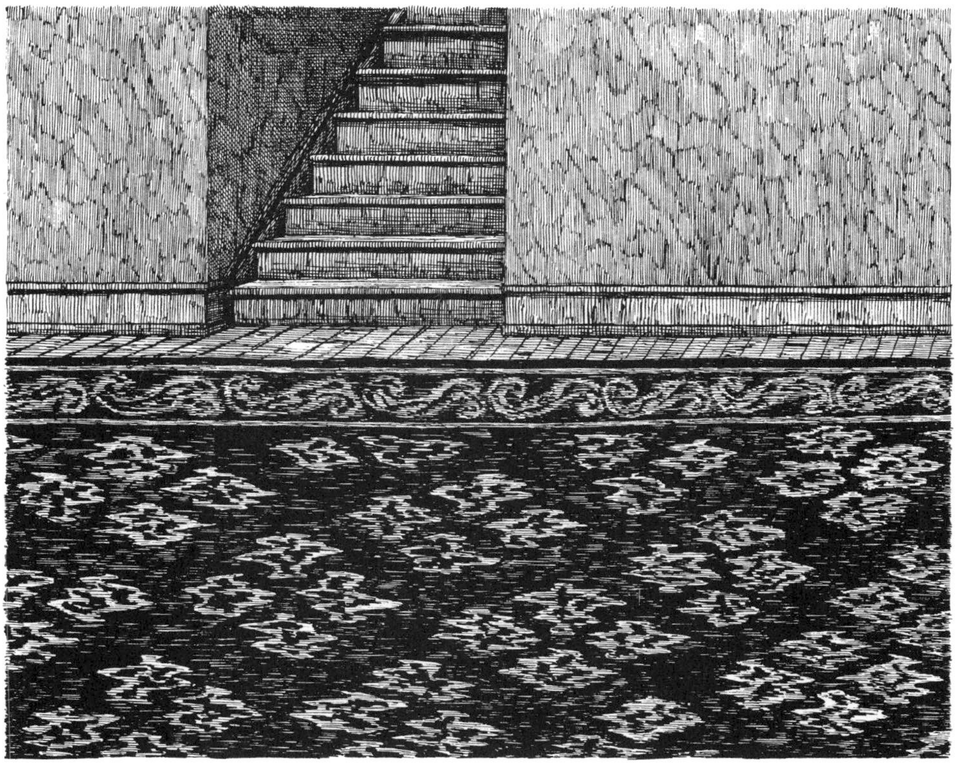

1.

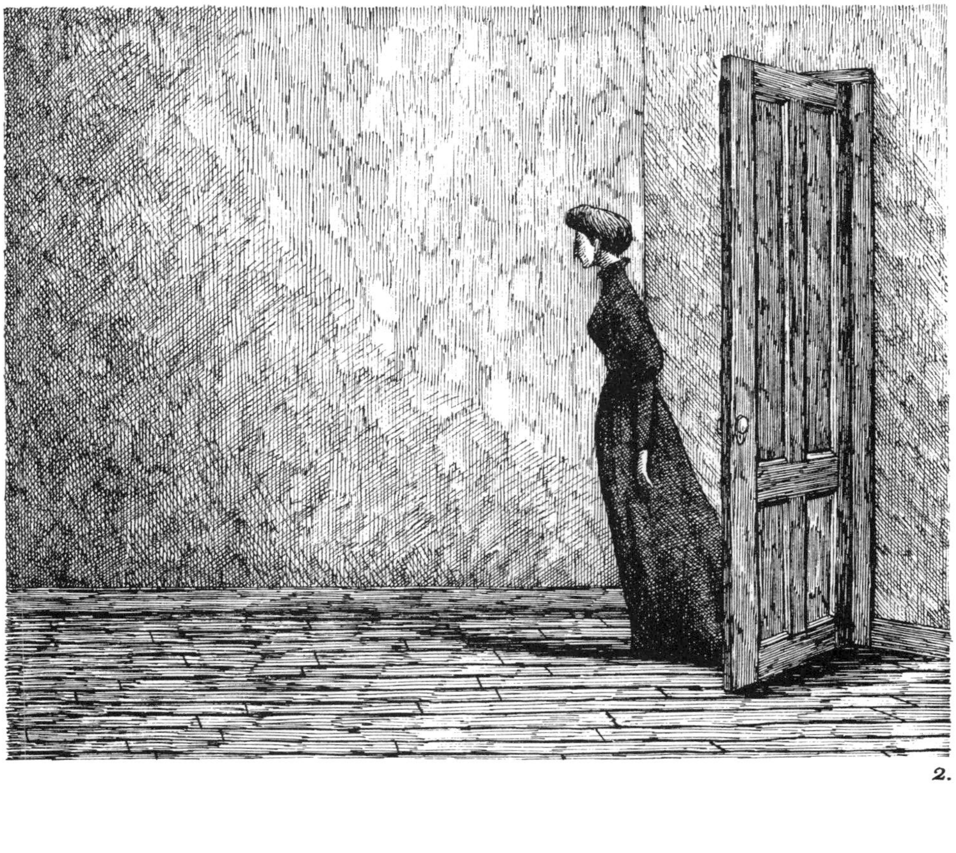

2.

3.

4.

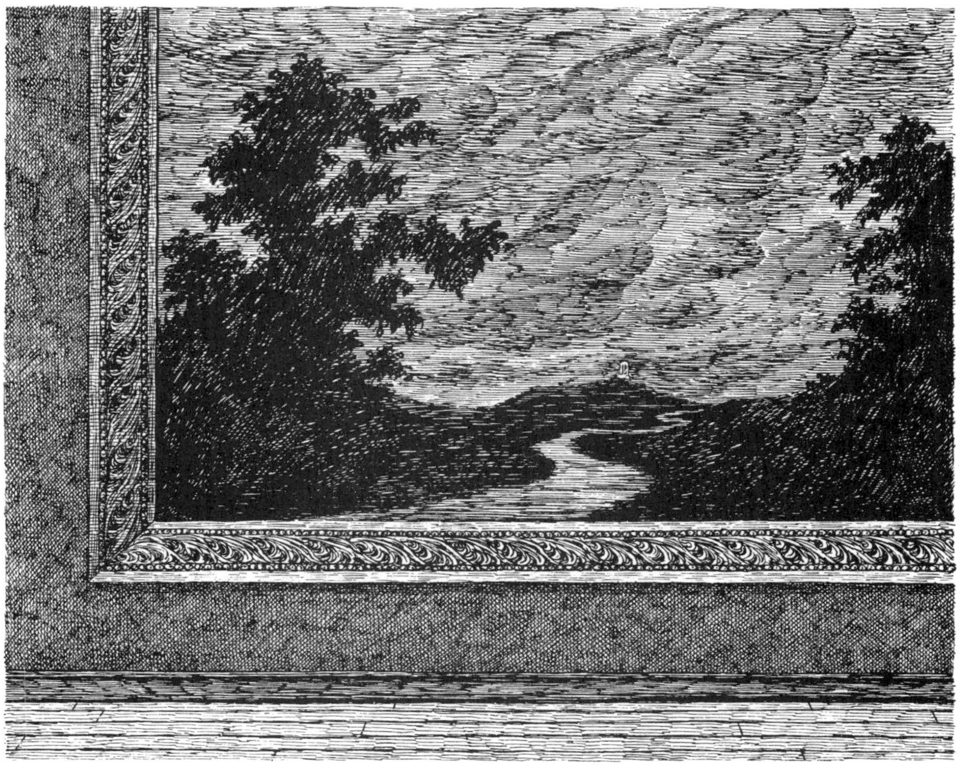

5.

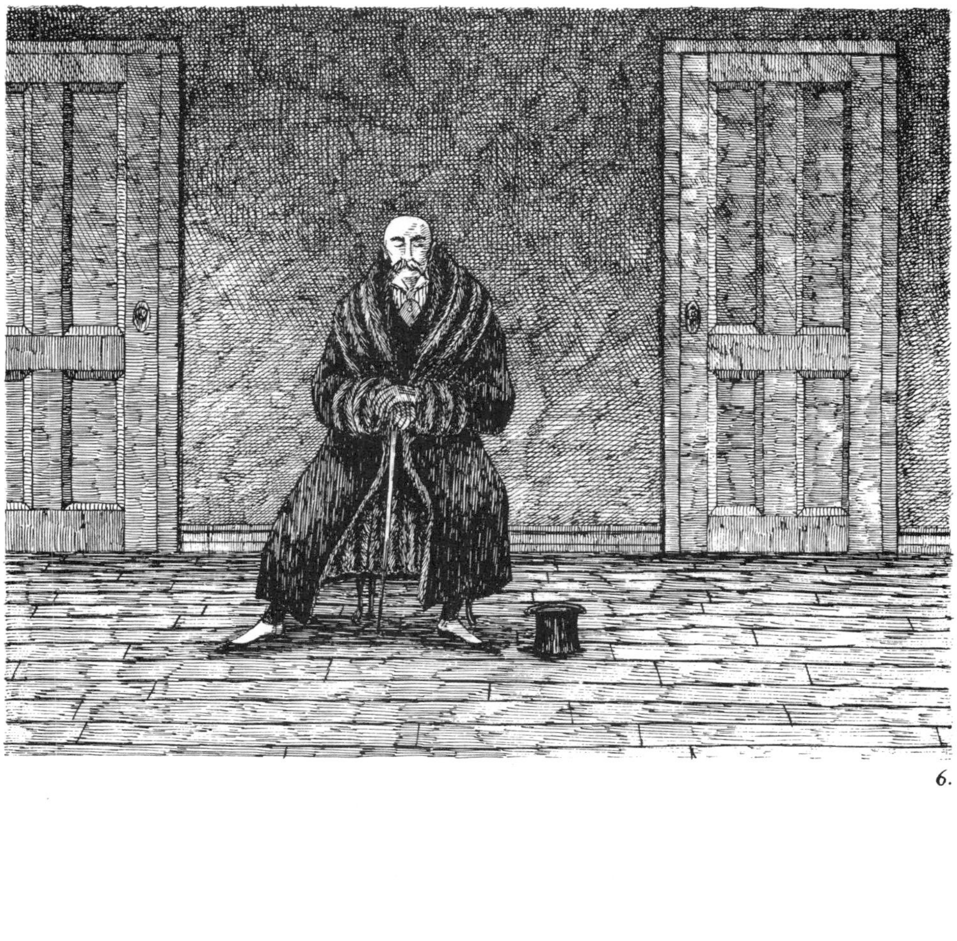

6.

7.

8.

9.

10.

11.

12.

13.

14.

15.

16.

17.

18.

19.

20.

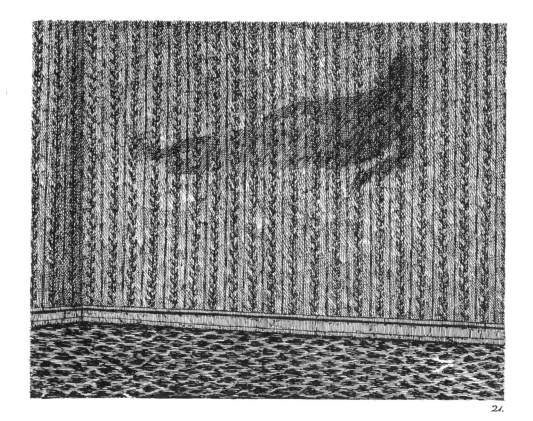

21.

22.

23.

24.

25.

26.

27.

28.

29.

U.

THE WUGGLY UMP BY EDWARD GOREY

Sing tirraloo, sing tirralay,
The Wuggly Ump lives far away.

It eats umbrellas, gunny sacks,
Brass doorknobs, mud, and carpet tacks.

How most unpleasing, to be sure!
Its other habits are obscure.

Sing jigglepin, sing jogglepen,
The Wuggly Ump has left its den.

We pass our happy childhood hours
In weaving endless chains of flowers.

Across the hills the Wuggly Ump
Is hurtling on, kerbash, kerblump!

When play is over, we are fed
On wholesome bowls of milk and bread.

Sing hushaboo, sing hushaby,
The Wuggly Ump is drawing nigh.

The moon is full: its silver beams
Shine down and give us lovely dreams.

Sing twiddle-ear, sing twaddle-or,
The Wuggly Ump is at the door.

It's making an unholy fuss;
Why has it come to visit us?

What nasty little wilful eyes
For anything of such a size!

How uninviting are its claws!
How even more so are its jaws!

Sing glogalimp, sing glugalump,
From deep inside the Wuggly Ump.

THE SINKING SPELL

O look, there's something way up high:
A creature floating in the sky.

It is not merely sitting there,
But falling slowly through the air.

The clouds grew pink and gold; *its knees*
Were level with the evening trees.

Morose, inflexible, aloof,
It hovered just above the roof.

It's gone right through, and come to rest
On great grand-uncle Ogdred's chest.

It settled further in the night,
And gave the maid an awful fright.

Head first, without a look or word,
It's left the fourth floor for the third.

The weeks went by; it made its way
A little lower every day.

Each time one thought it might have stopped
One found, however, it had dropped.

One wonders just what can be meant
By this implacable descent.

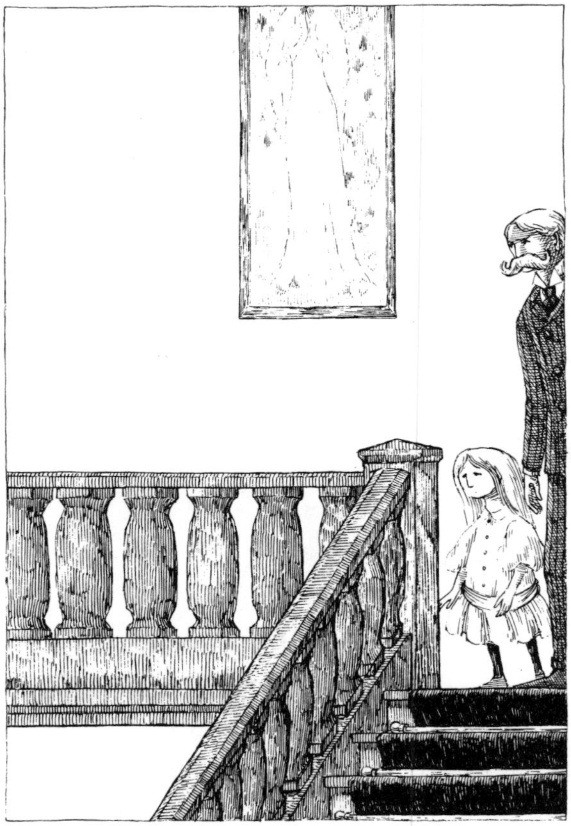

It did not linger, after all,
Forever in the upstairs hall.

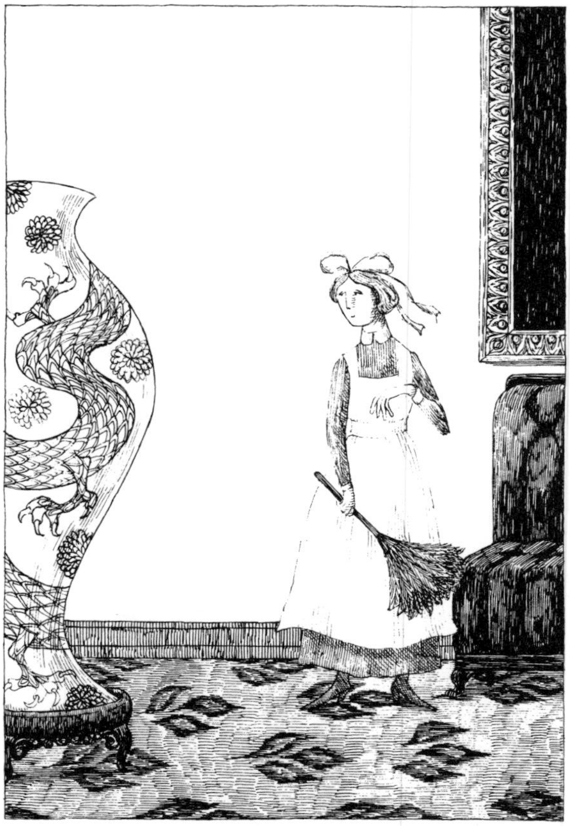

It found the drawing room in turn,
And slipped inside the Chinese urn.

It now declines in fretful curves
Among the pickles and preserves.

It's gone beneath the cellar floor;
We shall not see it any more.

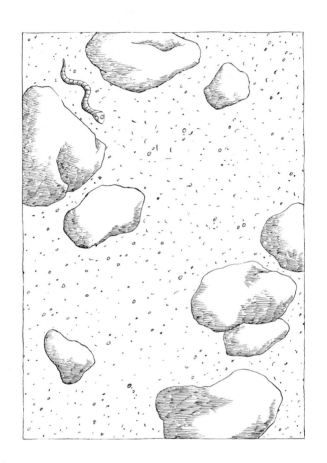

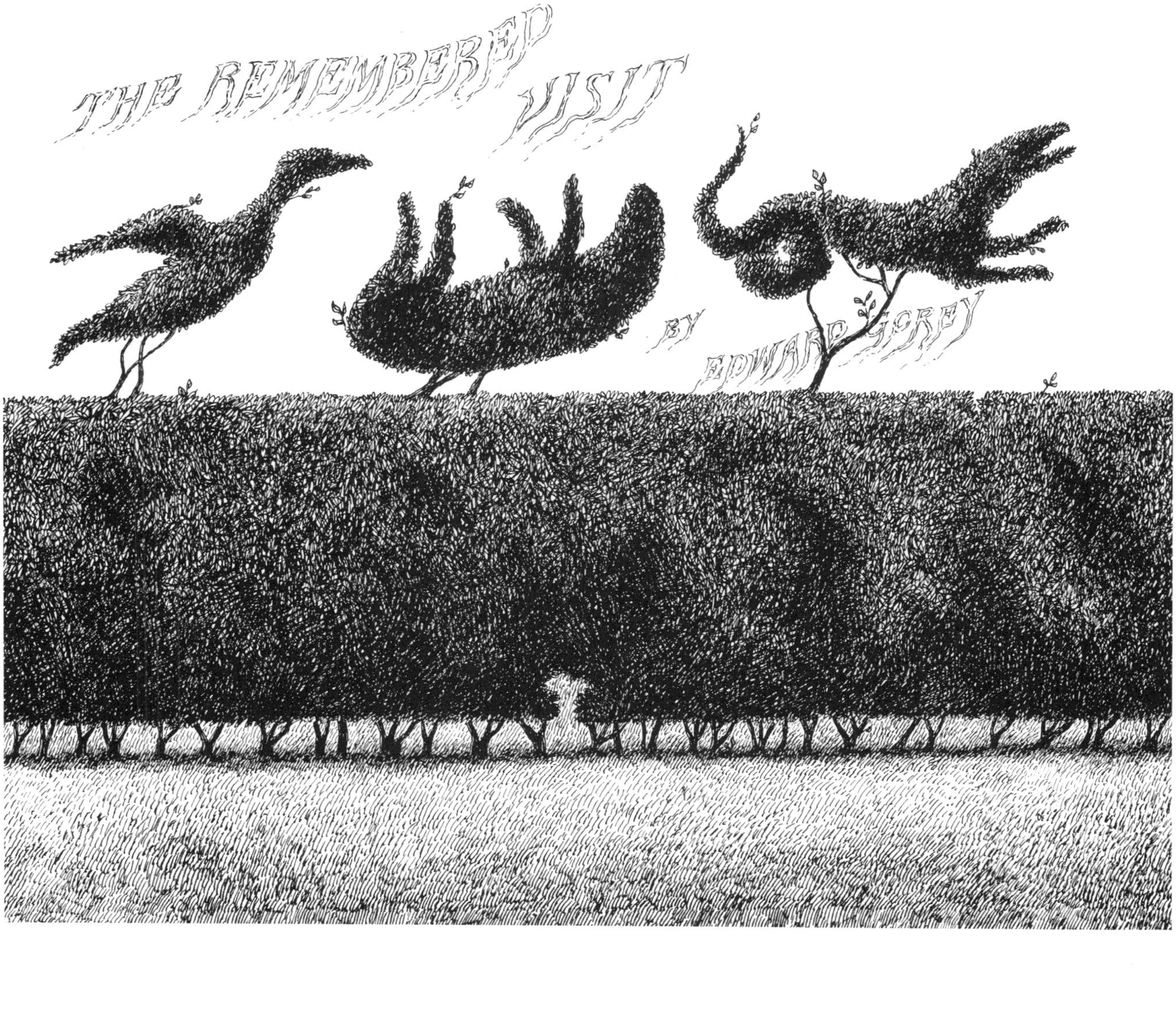
THE REMEMBERED VISIT
BY
EDWARD GOREY

The summer she was eleven, Drusilla went abroad with her parents.

There she climbed endless flights of stairs.

She tried to make out the subjects of vast dark paintings.

Sometimes she was made ill by curious dishes.

She was called upon to admire views.

When the weather was bad, she leafed through incomprehensible magazines.

One morning her parents, for some reason or other, went on an excursion without her.

After luncheon an acquaintance of the family, Miss Skrim-Pshaw, took Drusilla with her to pay a call.

They walked to an inn called le Crapaud Bleu.

They were shown into a garden where the topiary was being neglected.

Drusilla was told she was going to meet a wonderful old man who had been or done something lofty and cultured in the dim past.

Eventually Mr Crague appeared.

He kissed Miss Skrim-Pshaw's hand, and she presented Drusilla to him.

After they had sat down, Drusilla saw that Mr Crague wore no socks.

He and Miss Skrim-Pshaw mentioned a great many people who had done things in their conversation.

Tea was brought: it was nearly colourless, and there was a plate of crystallized ginger.

Mr Crague asked Drusilla if she liked paper.

He said he would have liked to show her his albums filled with beautiful pieces of it, but they were upstairs in his room.

Drusilla promised when she got home to send him some insides of envelopes she had saved.

Miss Skrim-Pshaw said it was time they made their adieux.

On the way back a few drops of rain fell. Somehow Drusilla was hungrier than she had been before tea.

Days went by.

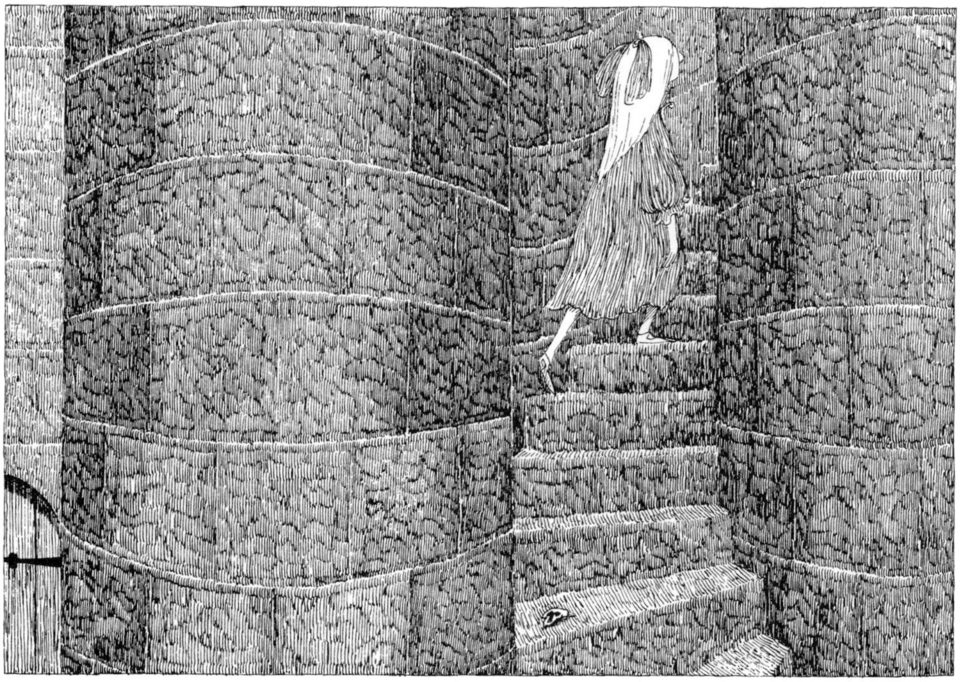

Weeks went by.

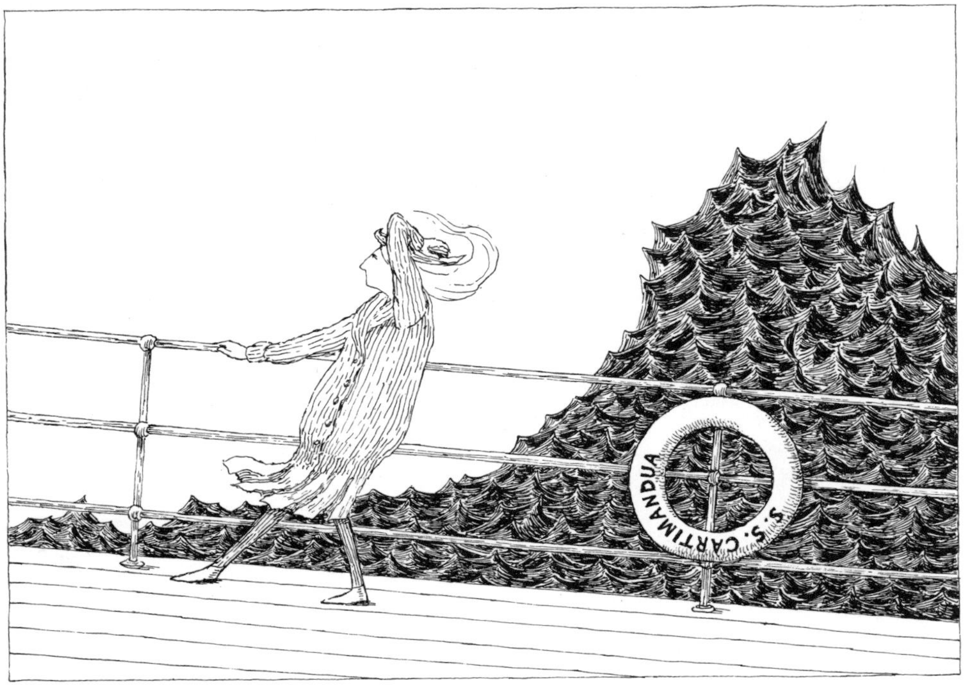
S·S·CARTIMANDUA

Months went by.

Years went by. Drusilla was still inclined to be forgetful.

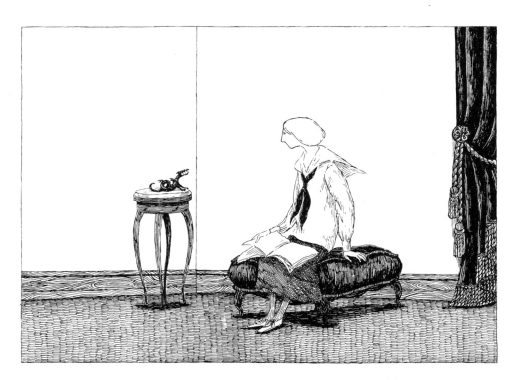

One day something reminded her of her promise to Mr Crague.

She began to hunt for the envelope-linings in her room.

*On a sheet of newspaper at the bottom of a drawer she read that
Mr Crague had died the autumn after she had been abroad.*

When she found the pretty pieces of paper, she felt very sad and neglectful.

The wind came and took them through an open window; she watched them blow away.

ALSO BY EDWARD GOREY

The Beastly Baby
The Nursery Frieze
The Pious Infant
The Evil Garden
The Inanimate Tragedy
The Gilded Bat
The Utter Zoo
The Blue Aspic
The Iron Tonic
The Osbick Bird
The Chinese Obelisks
The Epiplectic Bicycle
The Sopping Thursday
The Deranged Cousins
The Eleventh Episode
[The Untitled Book]
The Awdrey-Gore Legacy
The Interesting List*
The Admonitory Hippopotamus*

THE SECRETS

The Other Statue
The Night Bandage *et al**

WITH PETER F. NEUMEYER

Donald and the ...
Donald Has a Difficulty
Why we have day and night

WITH VICTORIA CHESS

Fletcher and Zenobia
Fletcher and Zenobia Save the Circus

DRAWINGS FOR

The Jumblies, EDWARD LEAR
The Dong with a Luminous Nose, EDWARD LEAR
Story for Sara, ALPHONSE ALLAIS
The Salt Herring, CHARLES CROS
Irene Iddesleigh, MRS AMANDA M'KITTRICK ROS*

**In preparation*